7 POWER PRINCIPLES I LEARNED AFTER SEMINARY

C. PETER WAGNER

From Gospel Light
Ventura, California, U.S.A.

PUBLISHED BY REGAL BOOKS
FROM GOSPEL LIGHT
VENTURA, CALIFORNIA, U.S.A.
PRINTED IN THE U.S.A.

Regal Books is a ministry of Gospel Light, a Christian publisher dedicated to serving the local church. We believe God's vision for Gospel Light is to provide church leaders with biblical, user-friendly materials that will help them evangelize, disciple and minister to children, youth and families.

It is our prayer that this Regal book will help you discover biblical truth for your own life and help you meet the needs of others. May God richly bless you.

For a free catalog of resources from Regal Books/Gospel Light, please call your Christian supplier or contact us at 1-800-4-GOSPEL *or* www.regalbooks.com.

Originally published as *7 Power Principles That I Didn't Learn in Seminary* by Wagner Publications in 2003.
Updated and revised edition published by Regal Books in July 2005.

Library of Congress Cataloging-in-Publication Data

Wagner, C. Peter.
[Seven power principles that I didn't learn in seminary]
Seven power principles that I learned after seminary / C. Peter Wagner.– Regal ed.
p. cm.
Originally published: Seven power principles that I didn't learn in seminary. Colorado Springs, Colo., Wagner Publications, 2000.
ISBN 0-8307-3803-7 (pbk.)
1. Holy Spirit. 2. Power (Christian theology) 3. Pastoral theology. I. Title.
BT123.W24 2005
234'.13–dc22 2005010406

1 2 3 4 5 6 7 8 9 10 / 10 09 08 07 06 05

Rights for publishing this book in other languages are contracted by Gospel Light Worldwide, the international nonprofit ministry of Gospel Light. Gospel Light Worldwide also provides publishing and technical assistance to international publishers dedicated to producing Sunday School and Vacation Bible School curricula and books in the languages of the world. For additional information, visit www.gospellightworldwide.org; write to Gospel Light Worldwide, P.O. Box 3875, Ventura, CA 93006; or send an e-mail to info@gospellightworldwide.org.

Table of Contents

Some Known Limitations of Seminary Training

For two or three generations, there has been an assumption here in America that clergy need to be educated on at least the undergraduate, and preferably the graduate, level in order to command respect in their communities and to serve their congregations as they should. Many traditional denominations still will not consider ordaining an individual unless he or she first earns a Bible college or seminary degree.

I must say that for generations the system worked fairly well. American churches, by and large, flourished, and throughout much of American history they constituted a vital sector of American society in general. The "minister," particularly in smaller communities, was expected to be among the best educated in town and, largely due to graduate training, was commonly esteemed on the level of attorneys and physicians.

This, however, is much less the case today. The change began to occur toward the end of the 1960s, when what were considered the mainline denominations began to decline in membership—a decline that continues today. Rather than "mainline," most people now see these denominations as "old line." Even the Southern Baptists, which for years were the rare exception, began to decline in membership in the late 1990s, the first time that had happened since the 1920s.

New Wineskins Replacing Old Ones

What is going on? America is experiencing a shift in the church-going population. The percentage of American adults who view themselves as born again or who are categorized as evangelicals has remained fairly steady. The decline in the old-line denominations has been accompanied by a proportionate increase in membership in newer churches. This is especially true among Americans born after 1960. Many children of parents who belonged to traditional churches are not joining their parents' churches.

For example, if you observe the churches in almost any metropolitan area of the country, you will find a number of churches that are growing vigorously, some of which are megachurches with several thousand members. By and large, these churches function very differently from the traditional churches in the city. Most of them do not belong to any of the old-line denominations, and even those that do have, for the most part, long-since been coloring outside of their standard denominational lines. The denomination usually tolerates them, at least in part, because of their substantial contributions to the headquarters' budget.

These non-traditional churches comprise what has become a new wineskin for the Christian movement. As in America, other parts of the world are experiencing similar phenomena. Many people call this movement the New Apostolic Reformation. It comprises the most rapidly growing segment of Christianity in our nation as well as abroad. In fact, researcher David Barrett divides world Christianity into six megablocks. His statistics show that the New Apostolic Reformation constitutes the largest non-Catholic megablock. Even more significant, the apostolic churches form the only megablock of churches currently growing faster than Islam.[1]

I regard this phenomenon as the most radical change in the way of doing church since the Protestant Reformation. The changes do not relate as directly to theology as they do to the way that the life of the church is played out day after day. Some of these changes include church names, leadership authority structures on both local and translocal levels, contemporary worship, ministry focus, financing of Christian work and prayer forms.

What is the difference between these apostolic churches and their more traditional counterparts? A major difference is the way in which church leaders, from senior pastors on down, are trained. If you check out the largest and fastest-growing churches in your city, chances are you will find that the majority of these churches are led by senior pastors who have never graduated from a Bible school or theological seminary.

The new seedbed for church leadership is now the congregation rather than seminaries and Bible schools. This is a positive trend, according to researcher Christian Schwartz. After an in-depth study of more than 1,000 churches in 32 different nations, Schwartz concludes, "Formal theological training has a negative correlation to both church growth and overall quality of churches."[2] In plain language, this means that the more degrees pastors have from seminaries and Bible schools, the weaker their churches are likely to be.

A notable difference between today's churches led by graduates of traditional seminaries and Bible schools and the newer leaders has to do with the theme of this book, namely supernatural power. I admit that I am overgeneralizing to make a point because many of those who have academic diplomas on their walls certainly minister in the power of the Holy Spirit as much or more than some newer leaders. Yet hardly any of them who minister in such a way learned to do so in seminary.

I consider myself an expert in the old wineskin. For 25 years I was an ordained minister in one of America's oldest wineskins—the Congregational Church. Let me explain.

Seminaries Do Teach About the Power of God

Five decades ago, I trained for ministry in what were then, and still are, regarded as prestigious seminaries, namely Fuller Theological Seminary and Princeton Theological Seminary. I am truly thankful for the theological education that I received in them, and I am well aware that I would not be where I am now without having received what they provided. But as I now look back at those seminaries and scores of others like them from a twenty-first-century perspective, it is clear that they were designed to serve what are now the old wineskins, namely the denominations. The seminaries that I chose were typical. Princeton, for example, was owned and operated by a traditional denomination, the Presbyterian Church USA. Fuller was independent, but nevertheless its mission statement, written in the 1940s, declared that it was founded with the purpose of serving the mainline denominations.

Did I learn about the power of God during the years that I studied at these seminaries? Yes, I certainly did. I learned, for example, that one of the attributes of God is omnipotence, meaning that He is all-powerful and there is nothing He is incapable of doing. He is powerful enough to create the heavens and the earth. I learned that He has power to save the lost and to transform us into new creatures in Christ Jesus. I sang, "There is power, power, wonder-working power, in the precious blood of the Lamb." I learned that He gives us power to overcome sin and to live holy lives. I learned that He is King of kings and Lord of lords.

Having said this, however, I later discovered that there were many other clearly biblical aspects of the power of God that were never so much as mentioned in class. For example, passages of Scripture such as John 14:12, "He who believes in Me, the works that I do he will do also; and greater works than these he will do, because I go to My Father," were, to all intents and purposes, ignored. If a passage like this ever did come up, my teachers promptly explained it away by saying that the "greater" miracle was not raising the dead or casting out demons, but rather seeing souls saved.

Why?

Warfield's Cessationism

In both of the seminaries I attended, my professors supported what is called "cessationist theology." The theologian to whom they referred as frequently as any other was Benjamin Breckenridge Warfield, a professor at Princeton Seminary in the early part of the last century. Warfield had been able to persuade a whole generation of Christian leaders that the supernatural works of God we read about in the New Testament were necessary only in the beginning stages of the Church. According to Warfield, after the apostolic age, particularly when the canon of Scripture was finally agreed upon, the miraculous acts characteristic of Jesus and the apostles *ceased*—thus the label "cessationism."

Back in those days, most of my friends and I used the *Scofield Reference Bible* as our scriptural tool. Although we knew better, we nevertheless ascribed almost as much validity to the study notes as we did to the biblical text. For example, one of the notes in reference to 1 Corinthians 14:1 read, "Tongues and the sign gifts are to cease,"[3] and we believed that to be the truth.

Elmer Towns sums it up as well as anyone:

> The typical systematic theology textbook in use in evangelical Bible colleges and theological seminaries in North America includes a passing reference to the reality of supernatural spiritual beings. The diligent theology student learns the devil is an angel who went bad, demons are the third of the angels who rebelled with him and the angels are the good guys that stayed good. A belief in spiritual beings remains a part of our orthodox view of theology, but there appears to be little interest on the part of theologians to apply this doctrine in any practical way.[4]

A Radical Paradigm Shift

This was my way of thinking during my first 20 years of ministry. I was trying to minister with one hand tied behind my back. Finally, however, I went through a paradigm shift and began to change my mind. I began to realize that I was under no compulsion to believe everything that I was taught in the seminary classroom. It took a while to be sure, but the changes were quite radical.

Here are several things that I now believe:

- **Understanding the modus operandi of angels and demons is a high priority for effective ministry.** It is true that I never denied angels and demons actually existed, but for all those years I had no idea how they operated in everyday life, let alone what to do about them.
- **Power ministries are vital for maximizing gospel outreach.** They include healings, miracles, prophecy, tongues, deliverance, spiritual warfare and other ministry activities. The biblical pattern shows that signs and wonders precede the most powerful evangelism.
- **Sources of information about the invisible world are not limited to the Bible.** Arriving at this conclusion was a major revision of what I was taught about epistemology in seminary. I firmly continue to believe that the Bible is inspired by the Holy Spirit. It is our principal and only inerrant source of information about the supernatural. What the Bible teaches cannot be contradicted. But the Bible is not our only source of valid information. For one thing, while God spoke through the Bible, He also speaks today. He frequently gives us new information. Even the dark side of the invisible world can provide us some valuable information, as long as we are careful to filter it through lenses of sanctified discernment, separating truth from falsehood.

What I have just described is the paradigm of most new apostolic leaders today. This is part and parcel of the new wineskin that God is shaping for the Church of the future. In 1996, I convened what was called the National Symposium on the Postdenominational Church. Over 40 leaders within the New Apostolic Reformation took the platform to express the way they were seeing the moves of God in the Church today. One of the panel leaders was Gary Greenwald, senior pastor of Eagle's Nest in Irvine, California. His panel dealt with the issue of supernatural phenomena in apostolic churches. I will not soon forget his words.

Supernatural Phenomena

Gary Greenwald said, "Most of you are here today because you are curious about the spiritual phenomena that are happening all around the world today. Our panel will be talking about things like drunkenness and laughing; people falling and shaking violently; outbreaks of miraculous healings; prophetic conventions where teams of men and women deliver personal prophecies to many; outrageous meetings where demons are manifesting and people are being set free; strange acts like strong winds suddenly blowing through congregations, blowing everyone's hair back, blowing individuals off piano benches; drops of oil falling inside buildings, everybody's Bible getting covered with drops of oil; people frozen in one position for hours, unable to move; and all kinds of other manifestations and phenomena."[5]

I fully realize that Greenwald's description of religious experience may be uncomfortable to many of today's Christian leaders who hold degrees from Bible colleges or theological seminaries. In fact, I can well imagine that some would relegate such behavior to the lunatic fringe. I know this firsthand because I went through my paradigm shift while teaching full-time at Fuller Seminary. When I began introducing some of these things in my classes at Fuller, I found myself under severe criticism. An unsuccessful attempt was even launched to force me off the faculty!

Let me be clear that not every church I associate with the New Apostolic Reformation operates within a philosophy of ministry that embraces all the apostolic power principles described in this book. The New Apostolic Reformation includes both charismatic and non-charismatic churches. I do not have hard facts, but my guess is that in America, perhaps 20 percent of the apostolic churches are traditional evangelical churches. Though few of these churches would be considered cessationist, they typically would choose not to feature in their day-to-day, week-to-week church activities the kind of outward, supernatural phenomena that Gary Greenwald describes. Many of them are growing vigorously without such manifestations.

God's Power in the World

However, outside of North America, particularly in third world nations, the percentage of new apostolic churches not outwardly practicing these power principles is most likely extremely small. For example, Mike Berg and Paul Pretiz spent years researching the fastest growing churches in Latin America, which turned out to be what they call "grass roots churches" and what I call "new apostolic churches." Almost all of the churches were pastored by leaders who had never been influenced by foreign missionaries and who had not attended mission-founded Bible schools or seminaries.

As part of their research, Berg and Pretiz contrasted these grass roots churches to the mission-related churches in Latin America, which tended to be more traditionally evangelical in nature and, generally speaking, were not growing like the others. Here is one of their significant conclusions:

> The real issue is whether mission-related churches can understand and adopt the best of a pre-Enlightenment worldview that is common to the masses in Latin America.

> This is a view that is open to the miraculous, to God's intervention in daily experience, to biblical confrontation with the demonic, and to a focus in worship that emphasizes reveling in God's presence rather than passive participation in a cerebrally oriented service.[6]

Today, some of the world's fastest growing churches are found in nations such as China, Nigeria, Indonesia and Brazil. Supernatural power in places such as these is the rule, not the exception to the rule. On a recent trip to Nigeria, for example, I met an evangelist who had lost track of how many people he had raised from the dead!

Looking Ahead

With this as background, let's now take a look at seven of the apostolic power principles commonly accepted and practiced in new apostolic churches—all of which I had to learn *after* graduating from seminary!

Notes

1. David Barrett and Todd Johnson, eds., *World Christian Trends* (Pasadena, CA: William Carey Library, 2001), p. 543.
2. Christian A. Schwartz, *Natural Church Development* (Carol Stream, IL: ChurchSmart Resources, 1996), p. 23.
3. C. I. Scofield, *The New Scofield Reference Bible* (New York: Oxford University Press, 1967), p. 1245.
4. Elmer L. Towns and Neil T. Anderson, *Rivers of Revival* (Ventura, CA: Regal Books, 1997), p. 219.
5. Gary Greenwald, statement transcribed from an audiocassette recording of the National Symposium on the Postdenominational Church, Pasadena, California, May 22, 1996.
6. Clayton L. (Mike) Berg and Paul E. Pretiz, "Latin America's Fifth Wave of Protestant Churches," *International Bulletin of Missionary Research* (October 1996), p. 159.

PRINCIPLE NO. 1

The Operational Role of the Holy Spirit

In new apostolic churches, day in and day out, you will discover that references to the person and work of the Holy Spirit are much more frequent than in traditional churches.

Why is this the case?

I think we have two underlying and closely connected reasons why this is true.

Focusing on the Future

The first factor has to do with focus. New apostolic churches are essentially driven by vision. There is a characteristic mind-set of apostolic church leaders that differs considerably from the mind-set we have become used to in traditional Christianity.

As we are aware, the traditional organizational structure for bringing churches together has been denominations. Denominational leaders tend to focus on the present and then draw from the past. Most denominations were founded by strong, visionary leaders. While they rarely used the term, they were, almost without exception, genuine apostles. The first generation or so of the denomination frequently turned out to be the most glorious generation in the denomination's history.

Following the normal sociological pattern of organizational life cycles, most denominations began to routinize after the first generation. The visionary, apostolic founders were generally replaced by administrators who, no matter how godly they might have been, typically saw their role as perpetuating the vision of the founder instead of casting new vision for the denomination. This is why I said that denominational leaders tend to focus on the present and draw from the past. When things slow down, they will frequently say, "We need to get back to our roots!"

The Vineyard Movement

I remember clearly the founding of the Vineyard movement in America back in the early 1980s. Its founder, John Wimber, was the person who most helped me to introduce the teaching of the power of the Holy Spirit into my classes at Fuller Seminary. We called our first course "MC510: Signs, Wonders and Church Growth." John's ministry of the miraculous was a powerful factor in the extraordinary growth of the Anaheim Vineyard Christian Fellowship of Anaheim, California, and he ministered in the same way in our Fuller classes. Despite (or perhaps *due* to) the vigorous opposition from several theologians on the faculty, attendance in the class broke all previous records.

Naturally, there was a close connection between what was happening at Fuller Seminary and the dynamic ministries of the Vineyard congregation that John Wimber was pastoring. In a short period of time, Vineyard churches were scattered across America and other parts of the world. Extraordinary miracles were reported on a regular basis, and the Vineyard became known as a vehicle through which God was restoring New Testament types of signs and wonders to the Body of Christ.

John Wimber was clearly the visionary apostolic founder of the movement. Many people consider the first generation of the Vineyard to have been the most dynamic segment of Christianity in the nation at the time. Yet the Vineyard today is not the same as it was in the 1980s. Two events changed its course. First, Wimber decided to structure the movement along traditional denominational lines rather than apostolic lines. Second, he died, which left Vineyard in the hands of second-generation leaders who did the best they could.

One of the outcomes of this was that the Vineyard left its position as being on the cutting edge of change and settled back into a more comfortable, maintenance-oriented mode. As I have said, this is not unusual for a movement of this type. The prominence of miraculous signs and wonders in many, if not most, of the Vineyard churches in America went into a notable decline.

Some years later, Vineyard leaders, lamenting the reduction in supernatural power in their churches, regrouped to make the changes necessary to bring it back. They decided that they could re-dig the wells of miracles by teaching a course at the Anaheim Vineyard called "MC510." The course, unfortunately, did not rekindle the fire of the 1980s.

My point is that the mind-set of the second-generation Vineyard leaders was typical of the ministry focus of denominational people. The focus begins with the present (not enough signs and wonders in our churches) and goes to the past (if we teach John Wimber's course again, we will get back to our roots and regain what we have lost).

The Focus of Apostolic Leaders

New apostolic church leaders have quite a different focus. They begin with the future and draw from the present. Their vision for the future is a God-ordained reality, not simply a desired possibility. They will, therefore, attempt to shape the present in any way possible so that the vision will be fulfilled. This introduces a dimension of what I like to call "consecrated pragmatism" into the mind-set of apostolic leaders, a trait that their more traditional counterparts often criticize.

Apostolic leaders characteristically will say, "We know where God wants us to go, and we'll do whatever it takes to get there!" They are convinced that the end, in fact, justifies the means. This does not signify that they will advocate immoral or unbiblical means to reach a given end, but it does mean that they are highly goal-oriented.

Reaching the Lost

This leads me to the second factor contributing to the high profile emphasis on the Holy Spirit in apostolic churches: the driving desire to reach out to the lost, which is part of the DNA of apostolic churches. Apostolic church leaders are not content with maintaining the status quo. They are future-oriented. They are sold out to advancing the kingdom of God by winning souls and multiplying churches.

The pragmatic question, then, becomes, What does it take to reach the lost? The answer, of course, is that it takes the power of the Holy Spirit. This is not simply a theologically correct statement. It has been borne out by empirical research. The churches that are growing most vigorously in the world are, with few exceptions, the churches that are permeated by the supernatural power of the Holy Spirit. Consequently, supernatural power becomes a determining operational force. It is derived from the premise that the Holy Spirit is the person of the Trinity most directly involved in effective evangelism. This does not mean that the emphasis on the Father and the Son is reduced in apostolic churches, but rather that the emphasis on the Holy Spirit is increased.

This is not only a pragmatic conclusion based on the premise that the more we have the operational power of the Holy Spirit the more we'll evangelize, but it is also understood as a clear biblical principle. While I was in seminary, I was taught that the Cross was an indispensable lens through which I should interpret the Bible. Before coming to a conclusion on any doctrine or important idea for ministry, I was taught to ask the test question, How does this relate to the Cross? The assumption behind this was that our focus should constantly be on the work of the Second Person of the Trinity—Christ. As I look back on this assumption years later, I regrettably feel that it ingrained in my mind an exaggerated Christology. The slogan "Christ is all!" has its positive connotations, but it can also become an obstacle to biblical evangelism.

Cross or Charisma?

For example, since graduating from seminary, I have met an increasing number of effective Christian leaders who do not question in the slightest that the work of Jesus on the cross is foundational to all that we believe and do, but who at the same time would not regard the Cross as the major compass point for moving ahead in active ministry. A much more determinative compass point for many of them is "charisma"—focusing on the

JESUS, HIMSELF, WOULD HAVE TAUGHT HIS APOSTLES TO CHOOSE CHARISMA—OR THE WORK OF THE HOLY SPIRIT—AS THEIR COMPELLING GUIDANCE FOR THE WAY TO DO MINISTRY.

active work of the Third Person of the Trinity while also affirming the Second Person.

As I have meditated on this interesting contrast between the Cross and charisma, it has become clear, at least to me, that Jesus, Himself, would have taught His apostles to choose charisma—or the work of the Holy Spirit—as their compelling guidance for the way to do ministry, such as evangelism.

Let me explain.

Recognizing Who Jesus Is

By the time of the events recorded in Matthew 16, Jesus' disciples had been with Him for a year and a half. Jesus asked His disciples what the people were saying about who He was. The disciples reported that some thought He was John the Baptist, and others thought He was Elijah or Jeremiah or one of the prophets. Jesus was obviously setting them up for the next question: "Who do *you* say that I am?" (v. 15, emphasis added). Peter, speaking for the group, responded, "You are the Christ, the Son of the living God" (v. 16).

This is an extremely important statement because it is the first time, after a year and a half, that the disciples were able to verbalize accurately that they recognized Jesus as the Messiah ("Christ" being the Greek for the Hebrew "Messiah") for whom the Jews had been waiting for centuries.

Why Jesus Came

Jesus then immediately replied, "On this rock I will build My church" (v. 18). This is the first time that Jesus ever mentioned the Church to His disciples. Why would He wait a year and a half to begin to tell them about the Church? Jesus, very simply, could not tell His disciples why He had come until they were sure they knew who He was.

Once He mentioned the Church, Jesus immediately told the disciples that building the Church would entail spiritual warfare. In the same breath, He went on to say, "The gates of Hades shall not prevail against it" (v. 18). Obviously, Satan and the gates of Hades would try their best to stop the growth of the Church, but they would not succeed. Why wouldn't they succeed? Because Jesus would give His disciples the keys to the Kingdom (see v. 19), which would open the opposing gates so that the kingdom of God could advance across the earth.

The keys that Jesus gave to His disciples would be "binding" and "loosing," terms directly related to spiritual warfare. The disciples must have remembered the earlier word that Jesus gave to them: "How can one enter a strong man's house and plunder his goods, unless he first binds the strong man? And then he will plunder his house" (Matt. 12:29). "Binding" means neutralizing the power of demonic forces, especially the power of those forces that attempt to stand in the way of spreading the gospel of the Kingdom throughout the earth.

The Shock: Jesus Was Leaving!

The disciples obviously received all of this, and they were undoubtedly affirming to one another that they would be more than ready to move forward with Jesus in order to expand the kingdom of God throughout the earth. What they were not ready for, however, was Jesus' next statement, namely that He would soon die and not be with them anymore (see Matt. 16:21). In other words, for the future extension of the Kingdom, Jesus' apostles would be on their own!

This shocking revelation was too much for Peter. He protested and argued with Jesus so strongly that Jesus finally had to rebuke him by saying, "Get behind Me, Satan!" (v. 23). It must have been quite a scene!

When things began to calm down, Jesus then explained to His disciples that, amazingly enough, it would be to their advantage if He left them. How could that be? How could anything be better than having Jesus present with them in person as they went forth to minister?

The Advantage of the Holy Spirit

Here is how Jesus explained it to them: "I tell you the truth. It is to your advantage that I go away; for if I do not go away, the Helper will not come to you; but if I depart, I will send Him to you" (John 16:7). The "Helper," of course, is the Holy Spirit. What Jesus was telling His disciples is the point I am trying to make now, namely *for the purpose of evangelization, the immediate presence of the Third Person of the Trinity is more important than the immediate presence of the Second Person of the Trinity!*

This is something I never learned in seminary. It is why some dynamic leaders of churches today choose the paradigm of charisma rather than the paradigm of the Cross to guide their ministry. They choose to focus on the operational power of the Third Person of the Trinity, just as Jesus instructed His disciples to do.

Jesus did spend another year and a half with His disciples. They received excellent training for ministry, not in a classroom working toward a degree, but out in the field learning by apprenticeship. By the time they finished, they had gained expertise in preaching, evangelism, morals, ethics, theology, Old Testament, prophecy, healing, deliverance, prayer, spiritual warfare and in many other areas. They had also received a commission from Jesus to go into all the world and preach the gospel to every creature (see Mark 16:15). No other group of people has ever been better prepared to aggressively spread the message of the kingdom of God.

However, Jesus made sure that His disciples understood that all this good training that they had received would not be enough. After His death on the cross and His resurrection, Jesus told His disciples that when He was gone, they should not immediately go out and start preaching the gospel. If they did, all their training would be for nothing. Instead, He told them to first "tarry in the city of Jerusalem until you are endued with power from on high" (Luke 24:49). The disciples had received the necessary education, but they had not received the necessary power, even though they had spent three years with the Son of God.

After Jesus had been with the disciples for 40 days following the resurrection, and just as He was ready to leave the earth at the ascension, Jesus reminded them of this once again. In what turned out to be His very last words on Earth, Jesus said, "You shall receive power when the Holy Spirit has come upon you; and you shall be witnesses to Me in Jerusalem, and in all Judea and Samaria, and to the end of the earth" (Acts 1:8). Fortunately, the disciples did what they were told and tarried in Jerusalem after Jesus left. On the day of Pentecost, they were filled with the Holy Spirit. Finally, they had the power to do what they were assigned to do.

The "Operational" Role of the Holy Spirit

I was, of course, taught about the Holy Spirit in seminary. I was taught that He is omnipotent, omniscient and omnipresent. I was taught to sing, "Praise Him above ye heavenly host, praise Father, Son and Holy Ghost!" I took a subject called "pneumatology," which is the doctrine of the Holy Spirit. But I was never taught how to tarry until I was endued with the filling and the power of the Holy Spirit, as were Jesus' apostles in the first century. In other words, I knew the *theology* of the Holy Spirit, but I was virtually ignorant of the present-day *operation* of the Holy Spirit.

While I was in seminary, there were people out there who were experiencing the power of the Holy Spirit in their lives and in their ministries. This made some of my professors quite insecure. They were so convinced that the Cross trumped charisma that many of my professors ridiculed these individuals as "holy rollers" or those practicing "hillbilly religion," as if they were on the lunatic fringe.

However, apostolic churches today are not at all embarrassed by frequent references to the immediate operation of the Holy Spirit in their sermons, their songs and their prayers or in general conversation among believers. They teach on the baptism of the Holy Spirit and the ministry of the Holy Spirit. They believe that all, not just some, of the gifts of the Holy Spirit are operating today just as they did in the Early Church. They frequently speak directly to the Holy Spirit and pray words to the effect, "Holy Spirit, we invite You to come and minister to us right now!" Numerous people are impacted so personally by the filling of the Holy Spirit that they look at the experience as a second blessing.

I see this as a very significant power principle, which has both biblical and practical justification. It is a major reason why apostolic churches today are winning more lost people to Jesus Christ than other churches. It is simply a matter of understanding and applying what Jesus meant when He said that the presence of the Holy Spirit is an advantage to those who desire to spread the gospel.

No amount of learning can substitute for ministry done by the operational power of the Holy Spirit.

PRINCIPLE NO. 2

7

Warfare Worship

In her best-selling book *Possessing the Gates of the Enemy,* Cindy Jacobs tells a revealing story. She was in a woman's meeting in which a member of the audience went up to the front of the auditorium with tears streaming down her face. She was suffering from a serious case of depression for which she had been hospitalized on occasion. Even at that moment, she appeared to be on the verge of another nervous breakdown. Though several other women gathered around her and started to pray fervently, there were no visible results. The symptoms continued. Then suddenly, someone called for a worship leader to come forward. Cindy continues,

> I went to the piano, and we began a type of warfare that is becoming quite frequent in prayer groups today—warring against the works of Satan by worshiping the Lord. . . .
>
> The women in the seminar stood to their feet. They sang; they clapped; they shouted; until suddenly the woman for whom they were praying began to weep and relate that the oppression had completely left her mind. It was as though a cloud had lifted, and for the first time in years her thoughts were clear. How we rejoiced together at the goodness of God on her behalf![1]

When I read about that incident, I could not help but realize how radically different it was from what the word "worship" had meant to me through the years.

One-Hour Worship Services

I took a course in seminary on worship and worship services. I was taught that the worship service should last no longer than one hour, and that, while there is room for a bit of variation, it usually contains three congregational hymns, one choir anthem, an invocation, a pastoral prayer, a benediction, a few announcements, an offering, a Scripture reading and a sermon. The congregation would usually be expected to stand for the invocation, the first hymn, the hymn just preceding the sermon and the benediction. (Of course, there would be more standing and sitting in liturgical churches.)

After graduating from seminary, my wife, Doris, and I went to serve the Lord as field missionaries in Bolivia. This is what I taught to church leaders during the 16 years that we were there. When I returned to the United States, the church I belonged to followed the same pattern. One hour a week was considered satisfactory worship for a normal believer.

Things are quite different now. The church I belong to, Springs Harvest Fellowship of Colorado Springs, features services that are up to two hours long. Praise and worship usually occupies the first 35 to 45 minutes. The people in the congregation are on their feet all that time, singing song after song, led by a worship band, a worship leader and worship singers on the platform. When worship is over, time is taken by announcements, greetings and sometimes a prophetic word. Then we move from worship to the Word, which is followed by an altar call for individuals in need of prayer.

Dynamic Participation in Worship

The first thing that impresses visitors from a traditional church to a new apostolic church like Springs Harvest Fellowship is that singing songs of worship and praise takes almost as much time as the entire traditional worship service used to take. The second thing that impresses them is that the audience seems to be drawn more deeply into dynamic participation in the worship compared to the routine performance in traditional services.

In most traditional churches, the congregational hymns are regarded as useful for preparing the congregation for the central focus of the service, namely the sermon. In other words, singing hymns is a means toward an end. In new apostolic churches, however, worship is different. True, the sermon is usually longer than in traditional churches, but new apostolic worship is not so much preparation for the sermon as it is a powerful spiritual experience on its own merits. It is not a means toward an end, but rather an end in itself. Church attendees expect the power of God to move on them as much (or even more so) during the worship time as it does in listening to the Word. Singing worship songs often connects them in heart and soul more directly with God than does learning about the Bible and the Christian life during the sermon time.

Worship interspersed, as it invariably is, with times of prayer becomes the expected opening for the power of God to come upon the people who attend church. The quality of worship, therefore, sets the tone for the whole service. In reality, the people end up more spiritually prepared for the sermon than in many traditional churches. This is why I include worship as one of the seven power principles in this book.

Worship as Warfare

I want to take this even one step further. The major effect of worship is often not on the worshipers themselves, drawing them closer to God (which of course it does). Rather, worship produces a strong influence in the invisible world. When God is glorified, His power and His light increase proportionately. Simultaneously, the forces of darkness in the invisible world can be pushed back and weakened through worship so that they will have less probability of obstructing the purposes of God here on Earth.

It is at this point that worship can become a powerful weapon of spiritual warfare. This is what gives currency to the term I use as the title of this chapter, "warfare worship." While many leaders of the New Apostolic Reformation have known that worship terrifies demonic forces, few have verbalized it as well as Chuck Pierce in his book *The Worship Warrior.*

Most books on contemporary worship that I have in my library deal with the function of worship drawing us into intimacy with the Father. This in itself is quite a step forward from the traditional concept of the Sunday worship service that I have described. I think we would agree that worshiping in order to become intimate with the Father is quite a bit more meaningful than worshiping in order to prepare for listening to a sermon. If worship does not produce intimacy, connecting heaven and Earth, it, to that degree, fails to accomplish its intended purpose.

Chuck Pierce knows and agrees with this principle. However, in his book *The Worship Warrior*, he makes a radical suggestion. Could it be that intimacy with God is not an end in itself, as most of the recent authors on worship assume? Could it be that worship is a means toward a further end? If so, what could that end be? Pierce suggests that it might be aggressive spiritual warfare with the purpose of advancing the kingdom of God.

The subtitle for *The Worship Warrior* clearly reveals this concept: *Ascending in Worship; Descending in War.* For Pierce, intimacy with God is essential. Without it, we should not engage in high-level spiritual warfare at all. His book raises the following two related questions:

1. Where in the heavenlies does this encounter with God occur?
2. What happens after intimacy is achieved?

To address the first question, it is worth noting that many authors on worship would say that intimacy occurs in the bedroom. My friend, John Wimber, frequently said, "God has called us to the bedroom, not to the battlefield." Chuck Pierce, on the other hand, would argue that our intimacy with God does not occur in the bedroom, but rather in the "Throne Room" in heaven. As to the second question, once intimacy is achieved in the Throne Room, we move out in the name of the Lord to conquer new territory for Him.

Chuck Pierce puts it this way:

> In the physical, or earthly, realm we tend to worship the human heroes of battle and add God as an afterthought. The typical scenario does not include worship as part of the battle plan; instead, worship comes in the form of thanksgiving *after a victory*. In spiritual conquests, the

> Almighty gets all of the praise, but we still see warfare and worship as two separate acts.
>
> Our understanding needs to expand. God is calling us to bridge worship and warfare. When we read the Bible, we find that God instructs us to *ascend* into the Throne Room in heaven, be *clothed* in His authority and *descend* in war. There is a *sound* of heaven that enables us to recognize, embrace and advance through this process. It moves us toward victory in accomplishing God's will on Earth.[2]

If this is true, it would be wise to take a look at some biblical examples of warfare worship.

The Church in Jerusalem

When the Church was first founded in Jerusalem, it engaged in warfare worship. Each day, the believers continued to meet together in the Temple, and they were seen as "*praising God* and having favor with all the people" (Acts 2:47, emphasis added). This resulted in effective evangelism because "the Lord added to the church daily those who were being saved" (v. 47). Actually, the disciples had been in the Temple ever since Jesus had left them. "And [they] were continually in the temple praising and blessing God" (Luke 24:53). The purpose of being in the Temple, for most people, was to worship God.

But there was more.

This temple in Jerusalem was the same temple that Jesus had cleansed some time before by driving out the money changers (see Matt. 21:12). My point is that when Jesus cleansed the Temple—a warfare act in itself—He quoted two Old Testament

Scriptures, both relevant to warfare worship:

- **Isaiah 56:7.** "My house shall be called a house of prayer" (Matt. 21:13). The word used for "prayer" in this verse is the Hebrew *tephillah*, which means "psalm" or "prayer set to music." It is another word for what we commonly call "worship."
- **Psalm 8:2.** "Out of the mouth of babes and nursing infants You have perfected praise" (Matt. 21:16). The children in the Temple who were crying out, "Hosanna to the Son of David," obviously a worship action, triggered this quote from Jesus. But in Psalm 8:2, not Matthew 21:16, we find the specific purpose of this "perfected praise." It was, interestingly enough, to "silence the enemy and the avenger." Warfare worship will do this. It will prevent Satan and his forces in the demonic world from accomplishing their evil purposes!

This early group of believers doing warfare worship in the Temple were, of course, what we would regard as biblical believers. However, it is important to keep in mind that their only Bible at the time was the Old Testament. It is safe to assume, therefore, that they were being guided in warfare worship by Old Testament teachings. I suppose that they would have been familiar with the following passages:

- **Psalm 22:3.** "But You are holy, enthroned in the praises of Israel." God inhabits or dwells personally in the praises of His people. The word used for "praises" is again the Hebrew *tephillah*, which we understand as "worship." This tells us that during worship, the immediate presence of God is expected to be stronger than when we do not worship. The early believers would have known this.

- **Psalm 149:5-9.** "Let the saints be joyful in glory; let them sing aloud on their beds. Let the high praises of God be in their mouth, and a two-edged sword in their hand, to execute vengeance on the nations, and punishments on the peoples; *to bind their kings with chains, and their nobles with fetters of iron;* to execute on them the written judgment" (Ps. 149:5-9, emphasis added). The italicized words are an Old Testament phrase that is the equivalent to the "binding the strongman" phrase in the New Testament (see Matt. 12:29). This would have given the early believers courage to know that their warfare worship in the Temple could actually neutralize the power of the enemy.
- **2 Chronicles 20:3-24**. The believers in the Temple had undoubtedly heard the story of Jehoshaphat, the king of Judah, when he came up against the powerful armies of Moab, Ammon and Mount Seir. Jehoshaphat was frightened (see v. 3). He thought he did not have enough power to withstand his enemies, and he had no idea what to do (see v. 12). But then the prophet spoke and said to Jehoshaphat, "The battle is not yours, but God's" (v. 15). Consequently, the king decided that his best strategy would be to engage in warfare worship: "He appointed those who should sing to the Lord, and who should praise the beauty of holiness" (v. 21). The next thing the king knew, his enemies had all killed each other, "and there were their dead bodies, fallen on the earth. No one had escaped" (v. 24). Jehoshaphat discovered that warfare worship really works!

- **2 Kings 3:7-15.** The kings of Israel, Judah and Edom were in trouble. They set out to fight the king of Moab, but all their armies with all their animals became stranded in the desert without water. They asked Elisha the prophet to help them. What did Elisha do? He commanded warfare worship by saying, "Bring me a musician." The result? "When the musician played . . . the hand of the Lord came upon him" (v. 15). God sent water supernaturally, and the king of Moab was defeated. The armies that won the battle won because of warfare worship!

Paul and Silas's Escape

The gospel had begun to spread from Jerusalem into Europe. Paul was in Philippi with his apostolic team. He cast a demon out, and the resulting uproar was so intense that Paul and Silas found themselves severely beaten and thrown into the inner prison with their feet in stocks (see Acts 16:16-24). There seemed to be no hope. Their skin was torn and bleeding, the floor was hard and filthy, they were stripped and cold, there was no indoor plumbing, and they were exhausted and totally immobile. By midnight the average prisoner would have moaned and groaned and dozed into a fitful sleep.

But not Paul and Silas. "At midnight Paul and Silas were praying and singing hymns to God" (v. 25). This was warfare worship at its best. The results? An earthquake suddenly came, all the prisoners were freed and the jailer later received Jesus Christ as his Lord and Savior (see vv. 26-33). Worship, once again, opened the way for God to accomplish His plan here on Earth.

Can Your God Help?

Not too long ago, I was ministering in Indonesia. One of my Indonesian friends, Daniel Hanafi, told me a story that is a present-day example of the power of worship warfare.

Daniel had recently made a mission trip to the Sundanese, one of the truly unreached people groups in Indonesia. Not only are the Sundanese unreached, they also are among the most fanatic, anti-Christian, Muslim peoples in Indonesia. Any Christian who goes among them is aware that he or she is in a life-threatening situation.

On this trip, God opened the way for Hanafi to make personal contact with a Muslim *imam*, the rough equivalent of a pastor. The imam told Daniel up front that he wanted nothing to do with Christianity. Daniel knew that he couldn't preach to him. They developed a cordial relationship, however, and at one point Hanafi asked the imam, "Can I sing?" The imam

THE MAJOR EFFECT OF WORSHIP IS OFTEN NOT ON THE WORSHIPERS THEMSELVES; RATHER, WORSHIP PRODUCES A STRONG INFLUENCE IN THE INVISIBLE WORLD.

agreed to that idea. So Hanafi first sang "This is the day that the Lord has made" and then "We bring a sacrifice of praise."

Remarkably, by the time Hanafi had finished worshiping God in song, the imam had begun to cry. He looked at Daniel with pleading eyes and said wistfully, "Can your God help?"

"Help what?" Daniel asked.

"We have had a terrible drought," the imam replied. "Our wells are drying up! Our cattle are dying!"

Daniel looked back at him with compassion. "Can we pray?" he asked, and the imam said, "Okay." Daniel began to sing "As the deer panteth for the water, so my soul longeth after thee." Sure enough, before the song was finished, the rain started pouring down! The longstanding drought was broken.

What were the results of this worship warfare? The devil began to lose his hold. The imam was converted, and he now commutes four hours every Sunday to attend church. Since then, three other imams plus 50 other Sundanese have become faithful Christians.

Testing the Missionary

Sometimes I wonder what would have happened if I had been taught warfare worship in seminary before I became a missionary to Bolivia. If I had, I might have seen things happen like Sam Sasser did. Sam Sasser, a missionary to the South Pacific, told me that he was the first missionary to visit one of the islands there. Following the right protocol, he approached the chief and asked permission to preach the gospel to his people. The chief said, "Yes, but first you must pass some tests." Sam agreed.

Twelve strong young men soon came out and challenged Sam to match them in certain feats of prowess, which Sam, being athletic, readily did. Then the chief said, "You have done well. There is one more test." At that point the 12 men started a pagan dance to the beat of drums, designed to call down the territorial spirit whom Satan had assigned to the island. When they had reached a certain frenzy, three young women suddenly entered the middle of the circle and also started to dance. In a short time, the three women began rising up, and before long they were dancing in the air about 10 feet off the ground!

The chief, with a wry look in his eye, turned to Sam and said, "Missionary, can your God do that?" After a pause, Sam said to the chief, "Sir, my God is not in the levitating business. But I'll tell you what He *can* do. He can make those girls come back down!"

With that, Sam turned his back on the occult display. He took a couple of steps, raised both arms toward heaven and began to sing loud praises to God. It wasn't long before the three girls came crashing to the ground! One of them even sprained her ankle in the process, and she was seen limping around the village for a few days afterward.

Sam Sasser understood warfare worship!

The chief turned to Sam and said, "Missionary, you now have my permission to preach the gospel to my people."

What a tremendous power principle!

Notes

1. Cindy Jacobs, *Possessing the Gates of the Enemy* (Grand Rapids, MI: Chosen Books, 1994), pp. 172-173.
2. Chuck D. Pierce with John Dickson, *The Worship Warrior* (Ventura, CA: Regal Books, 2002), p. 17. Italics in original.

PRINCIPLE NO. 3

Prophecy: Hearing the Voice of God

I was recently handed a list of the 10 greatest revivals in history and was asked to choose the revival that has most affected me personally. Without hesitation, I chose the Pentecostal revival, which began at the beginning of the twentieth century

How would something that happened over 100 years ago affect me? I wasn't even alive at the time. To my knowledge, none of my ancestors were Pentecostal. The church that I first joined when I was saved in 1950 was anti-Pentecostal. I served for 16 years as a field missionary under two mission boards, both of which would go so far as to dismiss missionaries if they were caught speaking in tongues.

A Radical Paradigm Shift

My paradigm shift was not one of those sudden fillings of the Holy Spirit that many of my friends have experienced. As I look back, I think that my paradigm shift took about 15 years to complete. I spent an important part of that time doing scholarly research on the Pentecostal movement and discovering that, worldwide and across the board, the hand of God seemed to be resting more powerfully on this movement than on other segments of the Body of Christ. I learned a great deal from my research, and I wrote a book in the early 1970s called *Look Out! The Pentecostals Are Coming*. One of my friends recently suggested to me that this book turned out to be prophetic, and I think he was right.

As I maneuvered through this long process and gradually came to understand and experience the power of the Third Person of the Trinity, my entire ministry soared to a new level that I could not have imagined previously. This is why I did not hesitate to choose the Pentecostal revival that began 100 years ago as the most important of the 10 greatest revivals in history.

Because this paradigm shift was so radical, I tried to carefully observe and analyze its various steps and phases. There were many new things I had to get used to. Some were easier than others. Many are described in this book. As I look back, however, it is clear that the most radical of the mental, spiritual and intellectual challenges that I faced related to the topic of this chapter:

God speaks directly to His people today!

Some would be surprised to find out that many intelligent, good-hearted, born-again Christians cannot come to believe this. They think that all of God's revelation to His people is in the Bible. For example, this is what John MacArthur, one of the most famous and respected Christian leaders in America today, sincerely believes. In 1992, MacArthur wrote a book called *Charismatic Chaos* in which he attempted to disprove many of the major distinctives of Pentecostals and charismatics. It is very significant that the title of his first chapter is: "Does God Still Give Revelation?"

MacArthur's answer to that question is the same one I would have given before my paradigm shift. His general thesis is No! God does not still give revelation. Here are his exact words: "Scripture is a closed system of truth, complete, sufficient, and not to be added to (Jude 3; Rev. 22:18-19). It contains all the spiritual truth God intended to reveal."[1]

Reformed Theology

This is good Reformed theology. It is the standard belief of the churches that have come down to us from John Calvin, John Knox and Abraham Kuyper. The two seminaries I went to, Fuller and Princeton, both identified themselves as Reformed seminaries. While I was in Princeton, I was taught that the doctrinal paradigm of the Presbyterian Church is molded by the Westminster Confession of Faith, which states:

> The whole counsel of God, concerning all things necessary for his own glory, man's salvation, faith, and life is either expressly set down in Scripture, or by good and necessary consequence may be deduced from Scripture: unto which nothing at any time is to be added, whether by new revelations of the Spirit or traditions of men (1:6).

Needless to say, prophecy was not a power principle that I was taught in either of the seminaries from which I hold degrees.

As previously mentioned, my seminary professors carried a theological label of cessationists, which means they believed that certain gifts of the Holy Spirit operated in biblical times, but *ceased* after the canon of the Bible was agreed upon. According to these professors, once we had the complete Bible, we no longer needed the ministry of the Holy Spirit through things such as healings, miracles, tongues, discernment of spirits and especially prophecy.

Jack Deere's Paradigm Shift

Jack Deere, arguably, has helped more people move from a cessationist paradigm to a power paradigm than anyone else because of the influence of his two major books: *Surprised by the Power of the Spirit* and *Surprised by the Voice of God.* He was actually dismissed from the faculty of Dallas Theological Seminary, a staunchly cessationist school, because he adopted the power paradigm that I am describing in this book. As a tenured professor, he found that he had to pay a considerable personal price for the change.

When Deere was writing *Surprised by the Power of the Spirit*, he was going to include a chapter on prophecy. But the more he studied it, the more he realized that the issues raised with prophecy merited not just a chapter, but a whole new book on the subject. In *Surprised by the Power of the Spirit,* Deere says, "The most difficult transition for me in my pilgrimage was not in accepting that Scripture teaches that God heals and does miracles today through gifted believers. The thing I resisted the most, was most afraid of, and which took the most convincing was accepting that God still *speaks* today."[2]

The New Wineskin

As I have already said, God has provided a new wineskin for His cutting-edge Church of the twenty-first century. With a few possible exceptions, the leaders of the churches of the New

Apostolic Reformation are no longer questioning whether God speaks to His people today. As I analyze the big picture, three characteristics of new apostolic leaders that relate to prophecy stand out in my mind.

1. New Apostolic Reformation churches accept the spiritual gift of prophecy.

Almost all of the new apostolic leaders I know will give a literal interpretation to the Bible verses that state God gives gifts of prophecy to certain members of the Body of Christ. Romans 12 and 1 Corinthians 12 are the two most detailed biblical passages on spiritual gifts:

- **Romans 12:6:** "Having then gifts differing according to the grace that is given to us, let us use them: if prophecy, let us prophesy in proportion to our faith."
- **1 Corinthians 12:1,7,10:** "Now concerning spiritual gifts, brethren, I do not want you to be ignorant. . . . But the manifestation of the Spirit is given to each one for the profit of all. . . . To another the working of miracles, to another prophecy."

The Gift of Prophecy

I believe that every Christian has the ability to hear the voice of God. As my paradigm shift progressed, I began to develop the ability to hear what the Holy Spirit was saying directly to me. I am sure that previously, the Holy Spirit had been leading me in ways other than speaking directly to me, such as by bringing certain circumstances into my life. However, I am now convinced that I was, at that time, operating under God's "Plan B." ("Plan A" is for each believer to be in such intimate relationship to Him through the filling of the Holy Spirit that He can literally communicate to us what is in His heart.)

When I was in seminary, no one taught me that prayer was ordinarily supposed to be a two-way process. None of my professors ever said something to the effect, "When I was praying this morning, God spoke to me and said so-and-so." The general idea was that we pray by talking to God and then wait until we see some visible evidence that God, in His sovereignty, has decided to answer our prayers. I will admit that this procedure does have certain validity; however, that is not all there is to prayer. Prayer should ideally be a two-way conversation between God and us. We speak to our heavenly Father and He speaks back to us, just as our earthly father would do if we were having a telephone conversation with him.

In my experience, the most challenging thing, once I believed that I could actually hear from God, was to be able to tell the difference between God's voice and my own thoughts. Since God doesn't often speak in an audible voice, this is something that each one of us has to learn how to do. I say "learn" because the more we concentrate on making it happen, the more it will happen. And learning is also a process. At the beginning you might not be very good at it, but over time your ability to distinguish what God is saying becomes more accurate.

I have now come to the point where, from time to time, God speaks to me so clearly that I can virtually say, "I quote." Granted, the quotes are usually my best paraphrases, but for the most part, they are pretty accurate. And, given my current position of leadership, some of these revelations from God are not relatively minor things (such as where I should go on vacation or if I should buy a new car) but influence fairly significant segments of the whole Body of Christ. Do I ever make mistakes? Sure I do, but that's part of the risk of stepping out in faith. To minimize the risk, I have a close circle of colleagues with whom I test these words from the Lord, especially if those words would affect other people. In doing this, I hopefully discover when I have made a mistake before it is too late.

Do I Have the Gift?

One of the reasons that I gave so much detail about my own experience of learning how to hear from God was to point this out: *I do not have the spiritual gift of prophecy!*

Those who have read my book *Your Spiritual Gifts Can Help Your Church Grow* will understand the important difference between Christian roles and spiritual gifts. Think about it for a moment. The Bible says, for example, that God gives to some the gift of faith (see 1 Cor. 12:9). But every believer, without exception, has a *role* of living by faith. There is a spiritual gift of evangelism (see Eph. 4:11). Not every believer is an evangelist, but every believer, whether he or she has the gift or not, has a *role* of being a witness for Christ.

This also applies to prophecy. As I just said, each one of us has a responsibility or a *role* to engage in two-way prayer and to hear directly from God. This is not a spiritual gift. However, God has chosen a few people to whom to give the spiritual gift of prophecy. Here is the way I define the gift of prophecy: The gift of prophecy is the special ability that God gives to certain members of the Body of Christ to receive and communicate an immediate message of God to His people through a divinely-anointed utterance.

This leads me to the second characteristic of new apostolic leaders that relates to prophecy:

2. New Apostolic Reformation churches also accept the office of prophet.

Some spiritual gifts, but not all, lend themselves to moving the gifted person into an office. When an individual has an office, it means that a certain segment of the Church has recognized the spiritual gift and has publicly authorized the person to use that gift for the benefit of the Body. It is helpful to understand that the gifts are given by the grace of God. Only God chooses who gets what gifts: "But one and the same Spirit works all these things [spiritual gifts], distributing to each one individually as He wills" (1 Cor. 12:11).

However, offices are not given by grace; they are attained by works. In other words, let's say that God gives someone the gift of pastor. That person is expected to use the gift, and then the fruit of that gift becomes visible to others. When the fruit of the gift, or the works, are sufficiently recognized, that person can then be ordained. This means they are given the office of pastor, not directly by God, but by the Body of Christ.

GOD'S "PLAN A" IS FOR EACH BELIEVER TO BE IN SUCH INTIMATE RELATIONSHIP TO HIM THROUGH THE FILING OF THE HOLY SPIRIT THAT HE CAN LITERALLY COMMUNICATE TO US WHAT IS IN HIS HEART.

Paul lists the office of pastor in addition to several other offices when he writes, "And He Himself gave some to be apostles, some prophets, some evangelists, and some pastors and teachers" (Eph. 4:11). We have grown accustomed to the offices of pastor, teacher and evangelist. However, new apostolic churches are now becoming more comfortable with the office of prophet (as well as apostle).

To be specific, some of those with whom I associate closely and who have been operating in the recognized office of prophet include Prophet Chuck Pierce, Prophet Jim Laffoon, Prophet Cindy Jacobs, Prophet Bill Hamon and Prophet Gwen Shaw. In fact, I have the privilege of meeting with all of them, plus around 15 more, once a year in the Apostolic Council of Prophetic Elders.

It is good that this power principle is being recognized more and more widely because prophets are part of the foundation of the Church. The Bible says, "[The household of God is] built on the foundation of the apostles and prophets, Jesus Christ Himself being the chief cornerstone" (Eph. 2:20). Now that this is taking place, God has begun to do things through His Church that surpass anything we have seen in history.

The third and final characteristic of new apostolic leaders that relates to prophecy is:

3. New Apostolic Reformation church leaders listen carefully to authentic prophecies.

The reason that God has provided prophets is so that His will can be heard, understood and obeyed by the Body of Christ. The major source of the revelation of God is, of course, the Bible, and no authentic prophecy could ever contradict what the Scriptures say. Nevertheless, there are many things that God wants to tell us today that cannot be found in the Bible. I believe this is why the Bible says, "Surely the Lord God does nothing, unless He reveals His secret to His servants the prophets" (Amos 3:7). Enscripturated biblical revelation is known by the Greek word *logos*, while contemporary revelation through prophecy is known as *rhema*. Because they are both the word of God, we must not neglect either one.

I use the adjective "authentic" to modify prophecy because, unfortunately, there are many spurious prophecies going around. In fact, because of some bad experiences with inauthentic prophecy, certain leaders have gone overboard and rejected the ministry of prophecy in general. In my opinion, this is a major mistake. Intelligent Christian leaders shouldn't reject prophecy any more than they should reject pastoral ministry because of some bad pastors or reject teaching ministry because of some bad teachers, both of which are all too common. Seemingly in anticipation of this, Paul writes, "Do not quench the Spirit. *Do not despise prophecies.* Test all things; hold fast what is good" (1 Thess. 5:19-21, emphasis added). In other words, one of the ways of quenching the Spirit is to reject prophecy, and we shouldn't do that if we want to obey what the Bible teaches.

How Does This Work?

Let me show you how this works with an illustration of one of my closest friends, Bill Hamon, who has both the gift of prophecy and the recognized office of prophet. He is the author of *Prophets and Personal Prophecy*, the book that actually helped me the most during my paradigm shift toward understanding prophecy.

First, listen to Bill Hamon's personal testimony:

> I have been moving in prophetic ministries since I was eighteen years old. I'll be sixty-two this summer, so it's

> been a few years. I can say, both honestly and conservatively, that over the last forty years I have laid hands on and prophesied over 30,000 individuals from all parts of the world. Many have also prophesied over me. At times I have prophesied for six, seven, or eight hours over two or three hundred people in one sitting. The anointing just seems to get going better and stronger the further I go.[3]

Hamon spoke these words while on a panel at a national meeting in 1996. Pastor Gary Greenwald, who was moderating the panel, introduced him as follows:

> Not long ago, I asked Dr. Bill Hamon to come to our church and to prophesy over the people. After he prophesied over three of my pastors, I decided to test him. I put a car salesman in the seat, and I said, "This is another one of my pastors." When Dr. Hamon laid hands on him, he prayed a bit in tongues, stopped and said, "Huh?" Then he prayed in tongues a little more, stopped and said, "Huh?" He said, "I don't know what kind of a pastor you are—all I can see are spark plugs, pistons, and a car that won't go!"

Gary Greenwald said, "The fear of the Lord came on me. I decided never to try to fool God's prophets again!"[4]

I can join Gary Greenwald in affirming Bill Hamon's accuracy. In 1992, Bill prophesied that Doris and I were going to relocate. I tried not to doubt the word, but I couldn't help it. We were in our early 60s and well settled at that point in our lives and careers. I was teaching at Fuller Seminary, and we had fully planned on finishing our lives peacefully in our comfortable home at the foot of the San Gabriel Mountains. But surprise! Four years later, we moved from California to Colorado, where we have remained ever since. When we moved, we had the assurance, through the prophetic word, that the move was God's plan for us.

As I write this, one of my major fields of ministry is serving as the founder and chancellor of Wagner Leadership Institute (WLI). WLI did not come about as a result of long-term planning. Even after we moved to Colorado, I continued teaching full-time at Fuller Seminary. I was very happy. I wasn't looking for anything else. Part of what I was doing was introducing the power principles described in this book into a traditional seminary, and I was seeing good results. I felt that cessationism was being relegated to the endangered doctrines list, if such a thing existed.

But then came another prophecy. This time it was from Cindy Jacobs, author of *The Voice of God*, at a birthday gathering for Chuck Pierce in my home. She spontaneously felt a spirit of prophecy come over her, and she prophesied at great length that I was going to start a school. Again, my first inner response was to doubt whether she was really hearing accurately, because never in my life had I ever entertained the thought of starting a school. However, it was only a month later that I resigned from my full-time position at Fuller, organized WLI and began our first classes.

Yes, God does still speak today. Hearing Him and obeying what we hear is an essential part of fulfilling our destiny here on Earth and being everything that He wants us to be.

Notes

1. John F. MacArthur, Jr., *Charismatic Chaos* (Grand Rapids, MI: Zondervan Publishing House, 1992), p. 51.
2. Jack Deere, *Surprised by the Power of the Spirit* (Grand Rapids, MI: Zondervan Publishing House, 1993), p. 212.
3. Bill Hamon, unpublished address given at the National Symposium on the Postdenominational Church, Pasadena, California, May 20-23, 1996.
4. Gary Greenwald, introductory address given at the National Symposium on the Postdenominational Church, Pasadena, California, May 20-23, 1996.

PRINCIPLE NO. 4

Miraculous Healing

When you fly to Maui, Hawaii, and approach the Kahalui airport, the most prominent landmark as you look down is the huge structure of King's Cathedral. What's more, if you are sick, you can go into that building during any of their weekend or midweek services and know ahead of time that you can receive personalized healing prayer.

Where Healing the Sick Is Routine

Pastor Jim Marocco is a longtime friend. I love the way that he forthrightly and unpretentiously obeys the Scripture: "These signs will follow those who believe: In My name . . . they will lay hands on the sick, and they will recover" (Mark 16:17-18). In Pastor Marocco's church, healing the sick is not something that is done from time to time, nor is it a low-key invitation to those who might choose to stay late after the service. It is just as much a part of what the church usually does at its regular meetings as are worship, prayer, welcoming visitors, the sermon, the announcements or taking an offering.

During the worship time, after singing a few songs, Pastor Marocco simply invites all those who need prayer for healing to come forward. Since everyone is standing anyway, it is not at all disruptive for 20 or more people to slip out of their seats and go up front. The entire pastoral staff is waiting there with small bottles of oil in their hands. While the band plays softly in the background, every person who comes forward is anointed with oil and prayed for according to his or her need. When that is over, the congregation resumes singing worship songs and the meeting goes on.

Normally, any number of reports will come in during the following week of substantial, verifiable healings that have occurred as a direct result of the healing prayer in the services. In other words, miraculous healing is a regular part of the ministry of King's Cathedral, and everybody in town—believers and unbelievers—knows it. It is little wonder that the church has been growing steadily for years.

Are Faith Healers on the Lunatic Fringe?

Praying for miraculous healing in church services is something that I did not learn in seminary. In fact, I recall that some of my professors would make reference to "faith healers" as if they should be included in the lunatic fringe. Somehow, the idea was planted in my mind that the reason we read in the Bible about Jesus and the apostles healing the sick was because medical science had not yet developed in those prescientific days, so miracles were more necessary at that time than they are now. Now that we have doctors and hospitals and health insurance and pharmacies, we have a much better way of dealing with sick people.

As a contemporary example, take the opinion of Professor Edward Gross of the Biblical Theological Seminary. In response to the question, Do miraculous gifts exist today? Gross answers:

> Both Scripture and experience answer a resounding no. Those who claim that such gifts are for today are wrong. In their zeal to promote God, they are teaching error. We must remember that error leads away from God. The Spirit of God, the Spirit of power, is also the Spirit of truth. One cannot sacrifice the truth without grieving the Holy Spirit.[1]

Gross, like the seminary professors who taught me, was strongly influenced by Benjamin Warfield, whom I referenced earlier. Regarding Benjamin Warfield, Gross states:

> B. B. Warfield was a devout theologian of the old Princeton Seminary. He was one of the finest biblical scholars of his day. He bravely defended the entire Christian faith against the many scholars who were denying it. . . . Warfield taught that the miraculous gifts of the Holy Spirit were not intended as permanent gifts of God to the church.[2]

Here is what Warfield himself said:

> My conclusion then is, that the power of working miracles was not extended beyond the disciples upon whom the Apostles conferred it by the imposition of their hands. As the number of these disciples gradually diminished, the instances of the exercise of miraculous powers became continually less frequent, and ceased entirely at the death of the last individual on whom the hands of the Apostles had been laid.[3]

A number of people today who read this quote from Warfield will be amazed that such things were actually being taught in our finest seminaries a generation or two ago, and that some are still teaching it. It is so far from the thinking and experience of today's cutting-edge pastors and other Christian leaders that it seems unbelievable. But it was certainly influential back then. During the first 20 years of my ministry, I must confess that I honestly believed that Warfield's position was true.

Preaching *Against* Miraculous Healing

As I have mentioned, Doris and I spent our first 16 years of ministry as field missionaries in Bolivia. I was strongly anti-Pentecostal at the time. I preached against the idea that God does miraculous healings today. I wrote articles against it. I couldn't have tolerated healing services such as the ones conducted at Jim Marocco's church.

For example, when Pentecostal faith healer Raimundo Jiménez came to our city from Puerto Rico, I strongly admonished my church members not to attend his open-air meetings where miracles were supposed to happen. My first disappointment came when I discovered that they attended anyway! That would have been bad enough, but I became extremely perplexed when some of them even testified to being healed! This, however, was only a temporary setback, because somehow I was able to rationalize it all away as some sort of clever deception—I had learned to do that in seminary.

Now, of course, my whole way of theologizing, interpreting the Bible, practicing ministry and teaching my students has turned around 180 degrees. I tell this story because, to a large degree, my personal paradigm shift is the story of a large part of the Christian Church over the last two or three decades. Granted, there are still a few pockets of cessationism here and there, mostly in the Western world. Edward Gross, whom I have cited, would be an example. However, generally speaking, most churches in most countries of the world pray for the sick and see miraculous healings on a regular basis. Many people choose to follow Christ because they have discovered that He cares for their bodies as well as their souls.

Evangelism with Miraculous Healing

We now live in the period of the greatest spiritual harvest that the world has ever known. The widespread ministry of miraculous healing found in churches all over the world has been one of the causes, not an effect, of this unprecedented wave of evangelism and Church growth. When Jesus ministered, He healed the sick as routinely and as predictably as Jim Marocco does today. When Jesus sent out His disciples to preach the kingdom of God, part of their message was literally to demonstrate tangibly that God has power to heal the sick. For example, when Jesus sent out the 70, He said to them:

> Whatever city you enter, and they receive you, eat such things as are set before you. And heal the sick there, and say to them, "The kingdom of God has come near to you" (Luke 10:8-9).

The Bible says that healing miracles actually *validated* the ministry of Jesus. Some might think that the ministry of the Son of God would need no physical validation, but apparently it did. When Peter preached his famous sermon on the day of Pentecost, he told the crowd that Jesus of Nazareth was "a Man attested by God to you by miracles, wonders, and signs which

God did through Him in your midst" (Acts 2:22). We can conclude that Jesus' ministry was more powerful *with* miraculous healing than it would have been *without* it. This is the reason He equipped and sent out His apostles to do the same.

John, of course, was one of those apostles. Years later, when he wrote the Gospel of John, he organized the whole book around seven of Jesus' miracles: changing water to wine, healing a young boy, healing a cripple, feeding the 5,000, walking on water, healing a blind man and raising a dead man. John also said, "Jesus did many other signs" (John 20:30). Why did Jesus do so many signs and wonders? According to John, there was one central reason: "These [signs] are written that you may believe that Jesus is the Christ, the Son of God, and that believing you may have life in His name" (v. 31). In other words, miracles pave the road to effective and fruitful evangelism.

Signs and Wonders in China and Nigeria

The greatest evangelistic harvest in history is now taking place in China, where it is reported that some 20,000 to 35,000 persons *per day* are becoming born again. Though no one knows the exact number of Christians in China, some estimate that it is 100 million, and I have even heard higher numbers.

What role do signs and wonders play in this remarkable harvest? One of the top experts on China, Carl Lawrence, reports:

> The single spark that started this prairie fire [in China] was signs, wonders and miracles. A report from the conservative Lutheran China Study Center on Tao Fung Shan, Hong Kong, concludes that 80 to 90 percent of Christians in rural China are the result of a

miracle of healing, casting out of evil spirits, or divine intervention, and of first-hand witness' testimonies.[4]

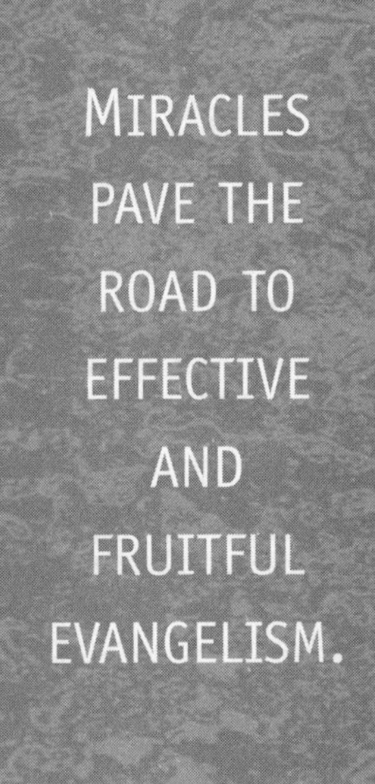

If China is the nation experiencing the greatest harvest today, Nigeria is probably the second. The last time I visited Nigeria, I participated in a small meeting of Nigerian leaders hosted by the pastor of Winner's Chapel, a church building with 50,400 seats, built on 630 acres of land. The choir loft of the church accommodates 1,000 people, and each of the three major wings of the auditorium is the size of two football fields. I attended a Wednesday night prayer meeting with no fewer than 6,000 people present.

But that was a small prayer meeting compared to the one I attended two days later at the Redeemed Christian Church of God Campground. This was an all-night prayer vigil held on the first Friday of each month in a facility that had the equivalent of 87 football fields under one roof. The leaders apologized to me for the low attendance that night—only 500,000. It ordinarily peaks closer to 1 million!

Why do I mention these extraordinary numbers? Simply to point out that Nigerian seminaries and Bible schools do not teach Benjamin Warfield's cessationist views. They take the Bible at face value when it says that these signs will follow every believer: "They will cast out demons; they will speak with new tongues; they will take up serpents; and if they drink anything deadly, it will by no means hurt them; they will lay hands on the sick, and they will recover" (Mark 16:17-18). For Nigerian believers, it is simply a matter of routine that when they pray for sick neighbors or fellow workers, they will actually see the miracles happen. As I mentioned earlier, I even met one Nigerian evangelist who has lost count of how many people he has raised from the dead!

Greater Works?

Apostolic churches, by and large, take a literal interpretation of John 14:12: "Most assuredly, I say to you, he who believes in Me, the works that I do he will do also; and greater works than these he will do, because I go to My Father." Gary Greenwald, whom I mentioned in the last chapter, tells this remarkable story:

> There was a boy by the name of Bree Farrow in one of my meetings. He was so skinny. He was yellow and jaundiced, and they told me that his liver was dead. He was twelfth on the national list to get a liver transplant, but they didn't think he would live until one was available. I prayed for him, and God's anointing came on me. The boy fell down crying. I walked out because I had to get to my next meeting.

> His aunt later came to me and said, "Bree went out jogging and skateboarding the morning after you prayed for him. He had so much energy! When he got back, he rode his bike all the way down to the beach. His color is all back. When the doctors took the tests, they said that his liver had regenerated. There was a brand new liver, and he has been released." He is totally healthy today, and God gave him a new liver by His miraculous power.[5]

Gary Greenwald told this story to 500 or 600 apostolic leaders attending the National Symposium on the Postdenominational Church in 1996. I was very interested to note that the audience reacted with applause, but without surprise. Virtually all of those apostolic leaders had seen miracles like this from time to time. Many could tell similar stories.

Miraculous healing is one of my favorite subjects because I see healing miracles on a regular basis. God has given me a special anointing for healing back and leg problems, but other healings happen as well. One of the most unusual occurrences happened when a young couple brought their five-year-old son to my office for prayer. The boy had been born with no ears and no ear canals. When I saw the boy, I must confess that my faith level dropped below zero. How could something like this ever be healed? I dutifully laid hands on the boy and prayed for God to give him ears, and I was not surprised when apparently nothing happened.

However, when the family was walking into a restaurant a half hour later, red bulges began coming out of the boy's head where his ears should have been. The mother and father looked at each other in disbelief. The ears did not grow out perfectly, but they did grow enough so that plastic surgery could be done and the boy could eventually hear.

Healing Teeth

Not everyone agrees how the passage in John 14:12, which states that those who believe in Christ will do "greater works" than Jesus did, should actually be interpreted. Certainly, raising the dead would be difficult to top. Hardly anyone would say that there is anything greater than regenerating lost sinners and making them new creatures in Christ.

Nevertheless, for several years now, dental miracles have seemed to attract a disproportionate amount of attention. I first met people whose teeth had been supernaturally filled when traveling with Omar Cabrera in Argentina during the 1970s. Since then, it has become virtually commonplace in Argentinean churches across the theological spectrum. You can visit almost any church in Argentina with a sizable congregation and expect to meet several people who will show you new fillings, replaced bridges and even new teeth that are growing in place of others that were extracted. In the 1990s, the phenomenon spread to Brazil where, unlike Argentina, the majority of the new fillings and crowns consisted of genuine gold!

I do not doubt that some readers may begin to question my authenticity when I make statements like this. Professor John MacArthur of the Master's College and Seminary says, "Frankly, I find all these accounts preposterous. It is difficult to resist the conclusion that that they are either utter fabrications or yarns that have grown with the telling."[6] But I would assure Professor MacArthur that I have visited Argentina and Brazil enough times over the past few years to be able to stake my reputation on affirming that dental miracles have truly been happening. A false report here and there, disproved by a dentist, is regrettable, but it must be seen as the exception, not the rule.

I mention this because, for many, it is more difficult to believe in reports of divine healing of teeth than reports of divine healing of cancer, especially if an ordinary silver filling is changed to gold, which has happened frequently. I once read a statement from a professional metallurgist, who is a Christian believer, stating words to the effect: "Don't underestimate this sign of replacing a silver filling with a gold filling. If it can be verified, then it is more spectacular to the scientific community than a virgin birth, medical healing, or even the parting of the Red Sea."[7]

A Challenge to Science?

Why is this? It is because scientists are unanimous in agreeing that only a nuclear reaction can change metallic substances, and this is always in the direction of changing a more expensive metal to a cheaper one. As far as a metallurgist is concerned, if it can be verified that mercury amalgam fillings have changed to gold, this is a sign that God has taken off the gloves with regard to the world of science and the world's preoccupation with it as the only source of truth.

This might well be what God has in mind. In 1 Corinthians 1:27, Paul says, "God has chosen the foolish things of the world to put to shame the wise." We live in a day when miraculous healing is definitely a feature on the Christian landscape. Seeing God's power manifested in physical healings is just as important today as it was in Jesus' time. It is common in other parts of the world, but I believe that churches such as Jim Marocco's church in Maui or the Chinese and Nigerian churches will also begin multiplying here in mainland America.

Notes

1. Edward N. Gross, *Miracles, Demons and Spiritual Warfare* (Grand Rapids, MI: Baker Book House, 1990), p. 71.
2. Ibid., p. 41.
3. Benjamin Breckenridge Warfield, *Miracles Yesterday and Today: Real and Counterfeit* (Grand Rapids, MI: William B. Eerdmans Publishing Company, 1965), pp. 23-24.
4. Carl Lawrence, *The Coming Influence of China* (Gresham, OR: Vision House, 1996), p. 67.
5. Gary Greenwald, introductory address given at the National Symposium on the Postdenominational Church, Pasadena, California, May 20-23, 1996.
6. John F. MacArthur, Jr., *Charismatic Chaos* (Grand Rapids, MI: Zondervan Publishing House, 1992), p. 132.
7. Source unknown.

PRINCIPLE NO. 5

Demonic Deliverance

In Jesus' mind, a normal assignment for His followers was to go out and spread the message of the kingdom of God by, among other things, casting out demons. He sent out the 12 apostles with "power over unclean spirits, to cast them out" (Matt. 10:1). He later sent out 70 disciples, and they "returned with joy, saying, 'Lord, even the demons are subject to us in Your name'" (Luke 10:17). Jesus then said, "These signs will follow those who believe: In My name they will cast out demons" (Mark 16:17).

Evangelism with No Deliverance?

If that was normal for Jesus, why isn't it normal for us? It is not unusual these days, for example, to observe a massive evangelistic event involving the expenditure of millions of dollars that attracts tens of thousands of attendees with no reports of a single demon being cast out.

There is little question that many people are saved during a typical mass evangelic event. However, research has shown that relatively few of those who come forward, sign decision cards and pray with evangelistic counselors end up truly converted, at least when measured by church membership. The research that I have done on mass evangelism indicates that the percentage of those who make first-time professions of faith in Christ at the event and those who subsequently become members of local churches runs from 3 to 16 percent. Even though we give thanks for those who are truly saved, most agree that this percentage is far too low. One possible explanation, though not the only reason, why so few people subsequently become members of local churches is because the demons that have kept these people in darkness are left intact to continue to do their evil work after the evangelistic campaign shuts down. Measured against Jesus' explicit strategy for evangelism, this methodology leaves something to be desired.

One major reason why this halfhearted biblical evangelistic methodology exists today is because a preponderance of today's Christian leaders were not taught in seminary that casting out demons could be a vital part of effective evangelism. When I went through seminary, I was taught to believe in the devil—our spiritual enemy No. 1. I was also taught that since the devil worked through the world and the flesh, we have to keep our guard up. But demons? No one taught me how demons behaved and what they did. I learned that in theory our enemy attacked through the world and the flesh, but I didn't get much information about the devil's modus operandi.

Consequently, I went out from seminary to serve the Lord in Bolivia without having a clue that I was entering an area where demons had had their way for centuries. Predictably, I didn't see a single demon during the 16 years that I was there! I'm quite sure now that they saw me and were very happy to keep me ignorant. They had little to fear, however, because if any of them had chosen to confront me, I probably wouldn't have known what to do anyway. This is undoubtedly one of the reasons why our years in Bolivia produced disappointingly little fruit.

All of this occurred before my paradigm shift. Since that time, I have come to realize that it is extremely important to know about and how to deal with the demons of various kinds that the devil employs to do his dirty work of stealing, killing and destroying (see John 10:10). This is a power principle that I believe we need to elevate, once again, to a primary position in evangelistic outreach, as well as in personal ministry. Jesus would consider it normal. Why shouldn't we do the same?

In Colombia, Deliverance Counts!

César Castellanos is the founder of one of the fastest growing megachurches in the world—the International Charismatic Mission in Bogotá, Colombia. The church has outgrown its facility, so for its seven services on Sunday, it leases an indoor basketball stadium that seats 18,000. At the time of this writing, they count about 50,000 cell groups in the church. Over 1,000 youth make professions of faith every week. How did this church grow to such gigantic proportions?

There are, of course, many factors that enter in to answer this question. A principal factor, however, is the systematic practice of demonic deliverance in the church. Hundreds of unbelievers get saved through the ministry of the International Charismatic Mission every week. Because of the dark spiritual atmosphere in Colombia, with widespread witchcraft and many other forms of the occult combined with rampant idolatry in the Catholic Church, an extremely large percentage of new converts are severely demonized. While it is true that in most cases demons are evicted when an individual becomes born again, it is equally true that in a considerable number of cases, all the demons do not leave. New believers need help. My friend Harold Caballeros of Guatemala says it well: "As any fisherman can tell you, when we catch a fish we need to clean it right away!"

Cleaning the Fish

César Castellanos makes sure that his fish are cleaned. As part of the package of accepting Christ and joining the church, every new convert is required to go away for a three-day spiritual retreat. One of the purposes of the retreat is to see that each person receives ministry of deliverance. The well-trained deliverance teams make sure that any demons that did not leave at the conversion experience are summarily cast out. Casting out demons in Bogotá is just as normal as Jesus thought it should be!

It is fairly easy to come up with examples like this from the third world. Deliverance played a key role in the amazing revival in Argentina, which was sustained for 17 years. Casting out demons triggered the 25-year process of transforming Almolonga, Guatemala, which is the only city so far that could clearly be considered transformed for Christ. Most churches in Nepal start with congregations made up entirely of persons who have been delivered from demons. These examples from third world countries could be multiplied indefinitely. However, we have few such examples here in the United States.

Let's Get with It in America!

In my opinion, this needs to change if we ever expect to see the true outpouring of the Holy Spirit that we have been praying for. My observation is that the ministry of demonic deliverance is at a very low level in American churches across the board. In every city in the United States, churches offer worship, counseling, youth programs, marriage retreats and 12-step programs for addictions, and anyone in the city is welcome to take advantage of these services and others. But too few churches in any American city that I know of offer the services of casting out demons. If the average person wants to be delivered from demons, they have no idea where to go for help. Unless we improve on this, we can have little expectation that our cities will be transformed. We can keep praying for this, but we will see few answers to our prayers if we don't begin to systematize demonic deliverance.

Can this happen? It all depends.

The Body of Christ is now in a better position for this than it has been in generations. Historically, the Body has had its ups and downs. At the beginning of the last century, Pentecostals began to cast out demons, but they were severely criticized by "respectable" Christians. Pentecostals then decided to become more "respectable" after World War II, so many of them no longer emphasized demonic deliverance as they had in the past. When the Charismatic Movement came along, it helped people to believe in demons, but it never mobilized them for action in the area of deliverance on a large scale. The Body was basically stalled!

Things Are Improving

However, things are improving. For example, when Frank Hammond's book *Pigs in the Parlor* came out in 1973, my friends at that time classified it as "ridiculous fantasy." However, my new friends now classify it as "groundbreaking." What a change!

Belief in demons has begun to go mainstream. Respected professors such as Charles Kraft, Neil Anderson, Tim Warner and Fred Dickason have helped greatly. Dynamic pastors such as John Wimber and Jack Hayford have moved us along. Seasoned missionaries who saw and practiced deliverance on the field became bold enough to begin to share their experiences with more traditional American congregations. As a result, growing numbers of American pastors now have a paradigm for biblical demonology, which they might not have had 10 years ago.

But even though an unprecedented number of American pastors now believe in demons, relatively few actually preach on it. Even fewer have installed a visible, local church deliverance ministry. How many churches, as part of their regular church program, teach their people how to cast out demons? The obvious answer is very few.

Why is it that so many churches ignore such a prominent biblical teaching? The first part of the answer to that question is because pastors, by and large, were not trained in demonology or deliverance in seminary or Bible school. While more and more pastors believe in demons, most really don't think that demons are much of a threat to the people in their congregations. Then there are some pastors who have chosen to avoid such "spooky" things for fear of alienating some of their church members. Bringing up demons would pull some out of their comfort zone. As an excuse, some pastors will say, "I believe in demons, but my congregation isn't ready." The reality is that most of the time the pastor isn't ready either.

What Have We Learned?

Nevertheless, the Church is making progress. Unlike 10 or 15 years ago, Christian leaders, for the most part, have now crossed the most formidable barrier to deliverance ministries. They now at least believe in the seven premises of basic demonology. In fact, some seminaries now teach them. These seven premises are:

1. There are such things as demons.
2. Demons are beings with distinct personalities.
3. Demons are active throughout the entire human population.
4. The intent of demons is evil—to cause as much misery as possible in this life and in the life to come.
5. Demons are organized under a hierarchy of leaders with Satan at the head.
6. Demons have considerable superhuman power through which they execute their wicked desires.
7. Demons have been defeated by Jesus' blood; therefore, they are vulnerable to direct confrontations empowered by the Holy Spirit working through believers.

We Need to Move Up a Level

While we may have come a long way, the Body of Christ is not yet at the level of demonic deliverance needed to sustain a process of revival or city transformation in our nation. We need to move from "Demonology 101" to "Advanced Demonology," so to speak. The sooner we do it the better!

Among some of those who have a basic paradigm characterized by the seven premises listed above, two widespread notions linger about demons and deliverance that, in my opinion, are much more than benign differences of opinion. They are actually *barriers* to allowing more people to experience true freedom in Christ. Unfortunately, they also significantly contribute to quenching the work of the Holy Spirit in our day.

What are these two harmful notions?

1. Christians Cannot Be Demonized

A major stumbling block to moving to a new level of demonic deliverance in America is the notion that Christians are immune to the type of demonic activity that calls for personal deliverance. Unfortunately, this is the official position of such a prestigious denomination as the U.S. Assemblies of God. One of their theology professors says:

> We do not believe for a moment that a believer can be demonized. But we do believe that a believer can become an unbeliever! We do believe that a man of faith can renounce that faith! When this happens, the possibility of demon possession is very real, for unbelievers can be demonized![1]

This respected teacher holds strong opinions about deliverance ministries in the Church. He goes on to say:

> It is unscriptural to lay hands on believers to cast out demons. Sincere but misguided people seek to do it, but they are wrong–very wrong![2]

Fortunately, not all Pentecostals agree. For example, Jack Hayford, one of America's most respected Pentecostal leaders, says:

> Demons do trouble and torment believers–and sometimes oppress them with burdensome bondage. Clearly, it would be improper to describe this oppression as "possession," but with equal certainty it would be foolish to deny the reality of the bondage. It would be worse

> to refuse or be unwilling to become equipped to minister to such soul-level affliction.[3]

I agree with Jack Hayford.

Why This Is a Serious Barrier

Why would the doctrine that Christians can't be demonized be such a barrier? The first reason is because it leaves us impotent to free many Christians from bondage and misery. My wife, Doris, has sustained a powerful ministry of personal deliverance for years. Her book *How to Cast Out Demons* is currently being used in many churches as a fundamental guidebook for deliverance ministries. She says:

> I pray deliverance only for Christians. I believe that a person needs the power of the Holy Spirit to maintain deliverance. From the testimonies of those whom I have prayed for, it is rather easy to maintain deliverance with the help of the Holy Spirit once the demon has been expelled. The testimonies sound quite similar and include statements like, "How wonderful it is to experience normal temptation that comes from the outside instead of the kind that rages uncontrollably from within and can't be withstood."[4]

Unbelievers, of course, can also be demonized, and Doris can cast out these demons. However, unless unbelievers are willing to be saved, the demons will return, often bringing more with them.

Pastors and Pornography

A few years ago, frightening statistics surfaced on the number of Christian pastors who are addicted to pornography. The availability of porn on the Internet has contributed greatly to this sad situation. In fact, the dean of Harvard Divinity School was terminated when it was discovered that he had loaded the computer in his seminary office with porn. Any deliverance minister will tell you that when an addiction like this is present, at some point along the way a demon or demons gained access, and their desire is to stay and use this addiction to destroy the person, as they did the Harvard dean.

Is there any help for those who have become addicted? In one year, I read six articles in Christian publications on the subject. Here were the suggestions for a cure in five of these articles: seek psychological advice, recognize your problem, confess your sin, clean up your life, find someone you can be accountable to personally, pray and fast, and seek counseling. No mention was made in any of these publications about the possibility of demonic activity!

WHILE MORE AND MORE PASTORS BELIEVE IN DEMONS, MOST DON'T THINK THAT DEMONS ARE MUCH OF A THREAT TO THE PEOPLE IN THEIR CONGREGATIONS.

But in the sixth one, an article by Mark Norris in *Ministries Today* went to the core of the problem. He told the story of a certain pastor by way of the following illustration:

> "I fasted, I prayed, I did everything I knew to do," the pastor said. "I made covenants and promises, whatever I could think of to end the battle. But the fact of the matter is, I didn't win the battle." Finally confessing to a minister who was adept in the area of demonic interaction, this pastor asked, "Can a Christian have a demon?" "Yes," the minister said, "they are here to be contended with." The ministering pastor instructed him to command the unclean spirit to leave in Jesus' name. "So I did; I just commanded the unclean spirit to leave. I didn't twirl, flip, choke or gag–nothing crazy," the pastor said. "But from that night until this afternoon, years later, I've never again had that bondage."[5]

Happily, this pastor found freedom. The sad part is that for each one who does find freedom, there are many, many more who do not because of the strange theology that Christians cannot be demonized.

The Effects of This Teaching

If Christians are immune to demonic invasion, as some contend, deliverance will naturally take a back seat for training leaders in seminaries and Bible schools. Such teaching will prevent local churches from developing effective deliverance ministries. Worse yet, it will actually force some believers to seek help elsewhere. In Mexico, for example, I have received reports that an alarming number of Pentecostal believers routinely consult witches in times of personal crisis.

John Eckhardt leads a powerful ministry in Chicago's inner city. The inner city area of almost any American city is clearly plagued with an above average presence of demons, and Eckhardt knows this very well. He becomes very upset with fellow Christian leaders who object to taking an aggressive approach to getting rid of demons. Here is what he says:

> Soon after I taught in our city a series on the subject of curses, there came forth ministries attacking the idea that many believers have curses over their lives that need to be broken. I had been teaching this series for a month and was seeing tremendous results. Many believers were being set free from curses and from the demons operating behind the curses. Nevertheless, there are many who teach that Christians don't need deliverance from demons.
>
> We have dealt with the opposition before and will continue to do so. However, this time an anger rose up in me to defend the truth: *Christians need deliverance* from curses and demons. The Lord was telling me that *truth must be defended.*[6]

2. The Belief That "My Way Is the Only Way"

The second barrier to seeing deliverance moving to new levels in America is a notion common among deliverance ministers that their way of doing deliverance is superior to all others. As an outsider, I am a bit mystified by this attitude. I know many deliverance ministers who use different methods, but the bottom line with all of them is that demons are evicted.

It seems logical to me that God would assign different ministries and activities to those who have the gift of deliverance. At least, that is what 1 Corinthians 12:4-6 sets forth as the rule.

This is necessary because demons are different, and the strongholds in individuals that invite demonic activity are also different. Some demons leave at conversion, some leave at baptism, some leave at a church altar call and some leave through a truth encounter. Some demons can be self-delivered, while others require a major-league power encounter before they will go. The Body of Christ needs different deliverance ministers who are equipped to handle deliverance at different levels and in different situations. I would say, the more variety of deliverance ministries the better!

I would also like to see a networking of deliverance ministers and ministries so that referrals begin to take place. The medical profession does it. An orthopedic surgeon would not attempt a heart transplant—the patient would be referred. The legal profession does it. An estate-planning attorney would not defend a client suspected of murder—the client would be referred. But apparently, we are not yet ready for this in the ministry of deliverance.

Retooling for Revival

Deliverance ministry is foundational for revival. I urge the American Church to place demonic deliverance higher on their priority list than it has been. Here are four things that would make a huge difference in our cities and in our nation if Christian leaders would determine to implement them:

1. Local churches should become the principal base for deliverance ministries across the country. Parachurch agencies should continue to do whatever they can, but they cannot be a substitute for local churches.

2. At least 10 percent of the life-giving churches in any given city should have highly visible, efficiently functioning deliverance ministries. I don't believe that every church could or would want to do this. But with 10 percent of the churches focused on structured, proactive, accessible deliverance ministries that maintain the highest levels of integrity and accountability, we would be tooled for city transformation.
3. Fewer euphemisms and more biblical language should be used. The Bible repeatedly refers to deliverance ministry as "casting out demons," and I believe that we will have greater success if we do the same. Contemporary terms such as "prayer counseling," "spiritual ministry," "freedom in Christ," "spiritual liberation" or "breaking bondages" have a degree of validity for entry-level communication, but all in all they have a much lower level of impact than the biblical terms. An outstanding example of a local church that offers deliverance ministry to the whole community is Spoken Word Ministries in Jacksonville, Florida. They also use straightforward biblical language about their ministry. Pastors Ardell and Kimberly Daniels run a large advertisement in the "churches" section of the Yellow Pages, announcing in bold, block letters: "WE CAST OUT DEVILS!" Such an in-your-face approach might stretch the boundaries a bit for most churches, but the idea behind it needs to be promulgated in whatever format is appropriate.
4. The army of deliverance ministers must be enlarged. Not only should the numbers of deliverance ministers

> be multiplied, but I also think we should develop broadly accepted certification programs for them, such as we have for CPAs, pharmacists or even beauticians. It also would help if we could devise ways and means of compensating full-time or part-time deliverance ministers.

With a view of implementing some of these guidelines, Doris and I organized the International Society of Deliverance Ministers (ISDM) in 2004. ISDM provides many benefits for legitimate, recognized deliverance ministers, furnishes a kind of accreditation or identity with certificates of membership and membership cards, and builds personal relationships among deliverance ministers. The annual ISDM meeting brings members up to speed on the latest developments in the field and provides expert answers to questions that might come up in some of their more difficult cases. The membership process is intentionally rigid in order to preserve the integrity of the group.

Positioned for Revival

I believe that we are now positioned for revival. We are at a place where we can boost deliverance ministries to unprecedented levels. If we decide to do it, I promise you that God will help us. After all, why did Jesus come? "For this purpose the Son of God was manifested, that He might destroy the works of the devil" (1 John 3:8). This is the river of God. He wants us to move with Him in destroying the works of the devil so that we can receive the great outpouring of the Holy Spirit on our land that God desires we should have!

Notes

1. Morris Williams, "Do Demons Have Power to Invade Believers?" *Power Encounter: A Pentecostal Perspective,* ed. Opal Reddin (Springfield, MO: Central Bible College Press, 1989), p. 184.
2. Ibid., p. 182.
3. Jack Hayford, "Demons, Deliverance, Discernment," *Ministries Today* (July-August 1999), pp. 22-23.
4. Doris Wagner, *How to Cast Out Demons* (Ventura, CA: Renew, 2000), pp. 36-37.
5. Mark Norris, "Pornography, Pastoring and the Internet," *Ministries Today* (May-June 1999), pp. 34-35.
6. John Eckhardt, *Moving in the Apostolic* (Ventura, CA: Renew, 1999), p. 79. Italics in original.

PRINCIPLE NO. 6

Powerful Prayer

In his important book *The House of the Lord*, Francis Frangipane teaches that the power of God for city transformation will be released as the pastors of a city perceive their churches to be congregations of one citywide church and begin to pray fervently together. He experimented with this in his home city, Cedar Rapids, Iowa. At the time, the state of Iowa was suffering from an 11 percent increase in violent crime. However, at the same time, the city of Cedar Rapids enjoyed a 17 percent *decrease* in violent crime. The FBI then classified Cedar Rapids as the safest city of over 100,000 people in the United States for its statistical year.[1]

This is just one example of *powerful* prayer. I emphasize the word "powerful" because not everyone recognizes the difference between powerful and more routine kinds of prayer. Some, in fact, assume that because all prayer is presumably good, all sincere prayers must be equal in God's eyes. To them, categorizing certain prayers as wimpy and other prayers as awesome is wrong.

Everyone Knows How to Pray

What was I taught about prayer in seminary? Frankly, I can't remember much about it. I know that the two seminaries I studied in did not offer specific courses in prayer while I was there. I was instructed on how to preach, baptize, counsel and serve communion, but I recall no lessons on how to pray or even on how to lead a prayer meeting. There was an assumption that prayer, indeed, was important for the Christian life, but it also was assumed that everyone knew how to pray well enough. Learning how to pray, in the minds of the seminary faculty, would somehow take care of itself.

I am just guessing, but one reason why prayer did not have a higher place in the seminary curriculum could well have been because my professors, by and large, were Calvinists by theological orientation. Calvinism takes a very high view of the sovereignty of God and stresses predestination. Calvinism, in other words, presumes that God has known since before He even created the world who we were and what was going to happen in our lives, and even if we would end up in heaven or hell.

Does God Ever Change His Mind?

I imagine that my Calvinistic professors would have had a hard time with the title of Brother Andrew's book *And God Changed His Mind*, to say nothing of the content. My professors, when they brought prayer up in their lectures, would teach that the essential function of prayer is to change those of us who pray so that we will be content to conform to whatever might be the predestined will of God. The idea that prayer could actually change the course of future events was not considered, much less the notion that God would ever change His mind.

As his book title suggests, Brother Andrew would disagree. His book begins with this revealing story:

Some time ago I heard two Christian women discussing the plight of hostages being held by Middle Eastern terrorists.

"I feel sorry for those poor men and their families," one of the women remarked, "but really, this is God's problem, not ours. We have to remember that He has already decided how their stories are going to turn out."

The other woman sighed. "Yes," she said, "but it's frustrating! It seems we're all being held hostage by the evil people in the world—the terrorists and dictators, the drug dealers, the criminals. . . ."

The first woman smiled and patted her friend's arm. "Well, that's how it *looks*," she said comfortingly, "but we know God has His reasons for allowing these things. Even when we don't understand those reasons, we can be sure that *nothing* happens outside His will."[2]

Brother Andrew responds:

As I listened, I felt indignation rising within me. I could barely control the urge to turn to them and say, "What's the matter with you? Why are you talking this way? You're not helpless! God has given you the power to change the situation! Why don't you use it? Why don't you pray?". . .

Those two very devout women were steeped in a false doctrine that has infected the thinking of an alarming number of Christians in our time. I call it—for lack of a better term—*Christian fatalism*. Without realizing it, these women had succumbed to a spiritual error that has all but neutralized their effectiveness as believers.[3]

Books like Brother Andrew's were not yet circulating when I graduated from seminary. Consequently, I spent the early years of my ministry functioning under the standard Calvinistic view of prayer. Naturally, I went through a routine of prayer on a daily basis as I had been taught, but I could report very few examples of dramatic answers to my prayers. Looking back, I would say that, yes, I prayed, but it was not *powerful* prayer.

Effective and Fervent Prayer

I now take a more literal interpretation of James 5:16: "The effective, fervent prayer of a righteous man avails much." "Effective" and "fervent" prayer is apparently not the same as prayer in general. There must be a kind of prayer that is more effective and fervent than other kinds of prayer.

One of the things that helped me understand the true dynamics of prayer was a chapter titled "If We Don't, He Won't" in Jack Hayford's book *Prayer Is Invading the Impossible.* Notice that Jack Hayford did not say, "If We Don't, He *Can't,*" because obviously God can do anything that He wants to do. But Hayford, in my opinion, has a much more satisfactory view of the outworking of God's sovereignty than we tend to learn from Calvinism. He believes that what God does or does not do can actually depend, at least to some degree, on whether we pray and on how we pray.

Here's how I think about it. True, God is sovereign and He can do anything He wants to do. The sovereign God, however, apparently has chosen to order His creation in such a way that many of His actions are contingent on the prayers of His people. It is as if God has a Plan A that He will implement if believers pray fervently and effectively. If they do not, He then has a Plan

B that He will implement. God's Plan A is obviously better than Plan B for all concerned. However, the choice, according to the design of our sovereign God, is ours, pure and simple.

Here is the way Richard Foster states it: "We are working with God to determine the future. Certain things will happen in history if we pray rightly."[4] This is extremely important for apostolic-type praying. It opens the door for us to be assured that prayer does make a difference beyond merely changing the person who prays.

How About "Open Theology"?

While we are on the subject, those interested in powerful prayer will be encouraged to know that in recent years a group of respected theologians has raised a significant challenge to traditional Calvinism. Brother Andrew's *And God Changed His Mind* was a book that accurately reflected what intercessors really believed and practiced. Professional theologians, however, neither read nor paid any attention to Brother Andrew because he didn't possess the academic credentials that they felt were necessary for serious theological dialogue. Much to the surprise of the theological community, however, a few years ago, some theologians who did have the necessary academic credentials began to suggest that Calvinism might have some serious flaws. They began to call their point of view "open theology."

The theological focus of open theology is to understand the very nature of God more clearly than people have in the past. Much of open theology directly relates to analyzing how prayer is intended to operate in God's design. Interestingly enough, the theologians started asking the same question that

Brother Andrew asked: Does God ever change His mind? The Calvinistic answer is No, of course not! A sovereign God could never change His mind! But theologians such as Gregory Boyd, Clark Pinnock, John Sanders and others have begged to disagree. In fact, Gregory Boyd's landmark book *God of the Possible* has a subtitle, *Does God Ever Change His Mind?*

Prayer Gave Hezekiah 15 Years!

Boyd cites the revealing case of King Hezekiah. Hezekiah was sick and near death. Isaiah the prophet came to him and, presumably speaking out what God actually had in His mind at the moment, said, "Thus says the Lord: 'Set your house in order, for you shall die, and not live'" (2 Kings 20:1). I say that this is a "revealing" case study because, presuming that Isaiah was an authentic prophet, God had clearly determined that Hezekiah would die of the illness that he had. The language used is clear whether in Hebrew or in English.

The fact of the matter is that Hezekiah did not die of that illness, even though God had said that he would. Why? The Bible tells us specifically that it was because of powerful prayer! "[Hezekiah] turned his face toward the wall, and prayed to the Lord" (v. 2). He pleaded for his life. He wept bitterly.

Isaiah then received another word from the Lord: "[Hezekiah], I have heard your prayer, I have seen your tears; surely I will heal you. . . . I will add to your days fifteen years" (vv. 5-6).

Some Theological Thoughts

Here is the way Gregory Boyd processes this true story. He wonders "how this could be true if God foreknew all that was going to happen ahead of time, as I had been taught to believe all my Christian life. How could God have truly *changed his mind* in response to a prayer if the prayer he was responding to was forever in his mind? How could Scripture say God added fifteen years to Hezekiah's life if it was certain to God that Hezekiah was going to live those 'extra' fifteen years all along?"[5]

John Sanders, another credentialed theologian, is very explicit about prayer. He says, "Our prayers can have an effect on God's plans. It makes no sense to say God grieves, changes his mind, and is influenced by our prayers, and also claim that God tightly controls everything so that everything that occurs [like terrorists abusing their hostages in Brother Andrew's story] is what God desired to happen."[6]

Every chapter in this book is sprinkled with theological points, but this chapter on prayer has more than the others. The reason for this is clear: If we pray, expecting that our prayers will make a difference, we need to know if this assumption is truly biblical. Does everything happen because God has predetermined it whether we pray or not? Or does God leave some things (not all things, of course) open-ended to be decided based on the obedience of His people?

As another example, let's look at the city of Nineveh. God told the prophet Jonah that the wickedness of the people in Nineveh had greatly displeased Him. He sent Jonah to proclaim, "Yet forty days, and Nineveh shall be overthrown!" (Jon. 3:4). This language is as specific as it can be. However, forty days came and went and Nineveh was not destroyed. Why?

The reason is because the people of Nineveh did what God wanted them to do. They fasted, humbled themselves and cried out to God in prayer. They said, "Who knows? Maybe God will turn around and change his mind about us, quit being angry with us and let us live!" (v. 9, *THE MESSAGE*). The result? "God saw what they had done, that they had turned away from their evil lives. He *did* change his mind about them. What he said he would do to them he didn't do" (v. 10, *THE MESSAGE*, emphasis in original).

If there is any doubt that this is the nature of God, listen to what God says about Himself: "At one moment I may declare concerning a nation or a kingdom, that I will pluck up and break down and destroy it, but if that nation, concerning which I have spoken, turns from its evil, I will *change my mind* about the disaster that I intended to bring on it" (Jer. 18:7-8, *NRSV*, emphasis added).

Apostolic Praying

I have spent many years as a member of traditional churches and, more recently, many years as a member of new apostolic churches. Because of this, it is fairly easy for me to highlight the differences between the two. Here are some of these differences:

- In traditional churches prayer is *incidental*, while in apostolic churches it is *central*. Some apostolic churches have taken prayer so seriously that they added a pastor of prayer to the church staff.
- In traditional churches prayer is *routine*, while in apostolic churches it is *spontaneous*. True, there are times in virtually all church services when prayer is routinely expected, but in apostolic churches we also hear, "Let's stop and pray" followed by unprogrammed prayer action much more frequently than in traditional churches.
- In traditional churches prayer is *occasional*, while in apostolic churches it is *frequent*. For example, during worship in apostolic churches, the worship leader will typically lead the congregation in prayer several times in one service.

- In traditional churches prayer is *passive*, while in apostolic churches it is *aggressive*. Answers to prayer are not surprises; they are expected.
- In traditional churches prayer is *quiet*, while in apostolic churches it is *loud*. During prayer in apostolic churches there is more vocal audience participation and the noise level is notable. At times, the entire congregation will engage in "concert prayer," in which everyone prays out loud simultaneously.
- In traditional churches prayer is *reverent*, while in apostolic churches it is *expressive*. People pray with their eyes open at times, they kneel, they fall on the floor, they lift their arms up and down, and they walk around. At times, they will actually lift their voices in a communal "victory shout" with everyone screaming at the top of their lungs and clapping their hands, accompanied by a loud drum and cymbal roll.
- In traditional churches prayer is *cerebral*, while in apostolic churches it is *emotional*. There is much more passion in apostolic praying. Some apostolic churches keep boxes of tissue under the seats because, more often than not, certain people will start weeping during prayer. After a prayer time, many release their emotions by applauding or even shouting.

Cutting-Edge Prayer in Your Church

It is true that not every new apostolic church rates a "10" in its prayer life. Most new apostolic churches, however, are moving up the scale—and some quite rapidly. While visiting apostolic churches across the country, I have observed five innovative prayer characteristics that, in my opinion, should be widely imitated. The churches that have these characteristics are setting the pace for raising the level of powerful prayer in our country. I hope that you will begin to incorporate these in your church, if you have not already done so.

1. The Office of Intercessor Is Recognized

Today's great global prayer movement began in the 1970s. One of the offshoots of this movement was the recognition of the gift and office of intercessor. We did not hear much about intercessors, per se, in the 1970s, but their profile began to rise in the 1980s and was pretty much in place by the 1990s.

Most new apostolic churches have organized ministries of intercession. It is not unusual when I visit a new apostolic church to be introduced to "Jane Simpson, one of our intercessors" or "Jack Stevens—he heads up our church prayer ministry." In some churches, special name tags are furnished to intercessors so that people who need prayer can easily find them.

For many years, pastors were not aware that certain individuals in their church had been called by God to stand in the gap for the church and its ministry to a much higher degree than was expected of the average Christian. This is partially due to the fact that, as I have explained, all prayer was considered more or less equal. Intercession was not thought of as a specific ministry, as were evangelism, music, teaching Sunday School, serving as a deacon or similar things. Fortunately, this has now changed, and powerful prayer has been released because intercessors are recognized and even honored for their ministry.

2. Prayer Teams Cover All Church Services

So many apostolic churches now have constant prayer going on during their services that they wonder how they ever functioned

THE SOVEREIGN GOD APPARENTLY HAS CHOSEN TO ORDER HIS CREATION IN SUCH A WAY THAT MANY OF HIS ACTIONS ARE CONTINGENT ON THE PRAYERS OF HIS PEOPLE.

without it. Charles Spurgeon was a pioneer in this area, and he often referred to a room in the basement under the platform of the church that was staffed with intercessors as his "spiritual engine room." Many pastors were aware of what Spurgeon had done, but generating that kind of committed, persistent prayer in traditional churches was not an easy task. One of the reasons for this was because pastors had little instruction as to how to identify and deploy intercessors in their churches.

This has now changed in new apostolic churches. In many churches, the intercessors are organized into one or more teams with committed leadership and a strong feeling that the fruit of the ministry of the whole church is dependent to a significant degree on their ministry of lifting up that particular service before God's throne. Often, the intercessors pray in a separate room equipped with a monitor on which they can watch the proceedings as they pray.

3. Preservice Prayer Is the Norm

In new apostolic churches in which the intercessors have their own room, the pastors and staff make it a habit to spend time in the room with the intercessors before they go out to lead the church services. In some cases, the prayer in the room is spontaneous, with intercessors walking around the room and praying out loud simultaneously. The staff simply enters the room and joins the group, praying out loud along with the others. Occasionally, one or two intercessors may approach the pastor, lay on hands and pray for God's special anointing for the service to come.

Other churches are a bit more organized. When the pastor and other platform persons come into the room, the intercessors drop everything and gather around the leaders. Sometimes the pastors are kneeling, sometimes sitting, and sometimes standing. Frequently, prophecies will come forth as the intercessors seek to hear from God. I know of many new apostolic pastors who would no more think of going into the pulpit without that impartation through prayer than they would think of going into the pulpit without a shirt.

4. Local Church Prayer Rooms Are Made Available

It is one thing to recognize intercessors, pray during the services and pray for pastors before they preach, but many churches are now going further and establishing local church prayer rooms for sustained prayer. These rooms, which are set aside solely for prayer, are comfortable, tastefully decorated and pleasant. Many have dedicated telephone and fax lines, and some are equipped with computers connected to the church's website. Most intercessors use the prayer rooms for focused prayer for their own congregation and community, but increasing numbers are connecting to other prayer rooms in the nation and with prayer networks around the globe through the World Prayer Center.

The ideal of most local church prayer rooms is to have 24-hour prayer, seven days a week. This takes awhile to attain, but as a starter, the regular hours for the prayer rooms can posted each day so that church members and others in the community who need prayer know when they can call. Two recent books that are extremely helpful to those who are interested in starting local church prayer rooms are *Making Room to Pray* by Terry Teykl and *How to Have a Dynamic Church Prayer Ministry* by Jill Griffith.

5. Pastor Prayer Partners Are Utilized

I can safely say that more pastors have testified to me that their lives and ministries have been lifted up to a higher level through building teams of personal prayer partners than any other single cause. This is why I have said many times that of all the books I have written, *Prayer Shield* is the most important one for pastors. Whenever a layperson comes up to me in a conference and asks, "Peter, which of your books would you say I should take home to my pastor as a gift?" I always suggest *Prayer Shield.*

Unfortunately, once intercessors begin to be recognized as such, immaturity and lack of experience can cause many problems that begin to build barriers between some pastors and intercessors. *Prayer Shield* faces these barriers realistically and helps pastors and intercessors understand and appreciate each other. Once pastors and intercessors get on the same page, unprecedented spiritual power almost inevitably begins to flow into the pastor's life and ministry. The intercessors win, the pastors win, the church wins, and the future becomes brighter.

Other books that I highly recommend for helping pastors recruit prayer partners are *Your Pastor: Preyed on or Prayed For* by Terry Teykl and *Partners in Prayer* by John Maxwell.

The Power of Strategic Intercession

Ongoing personal intercession for leaders is extremely important, but there is yet another level that I refer to as "strategic intercession." Personal intercession can assure God's destiny for a certain individual. Strategic intercession can affect the unfolding of history. I quoted Richard Foster earlier: "We are working with God to determine the future. Certain things will happen in history if we pray rightly."[7] Walter Wink was even more effusive when he said, "History belongs to the intercessors!"[8]

Let's look at intercession a bit more closely. We often use the word "intercession" as a synonym for "prayer." In ordinary conversation, it is acceptable to use the words interchangeably, but not when we are dealing with them as technical terms. Prayer, of course, means speaking to God. Intercession, however, is coming to God specifically on behalf of another. All intercession is prayer, but not all prayer is intercession.

The word "intercession" is derived from the Latin *inter*, meaning "between," and *cedere*, meaning "to go." Intercession, then, is going between or standing in the gap.

The phrase "standing in the gap" comes from Ezekiel 22:30. This Scripture clearly shows how powerful strategic intercession can be. God was upset with His people because they "have used oppressions, committed robbery, and mistreated the poor and needy; and they wrongfully oppress the stranger" (v. 29).

What was God's Plan A for the situation? "I sought for a man among them who would make a wall, and stand in the gap before Me on behalf of the land, that I should not destroy it; but I found no one" (v. 30). The clear implication is that a strategic intercessor, at that point in time, would have made all the difference in the world. Since, regrettably, there was no intercessor, God went to His Plan B. "I have poured out My indignation on them; I have consumed them with the fire of My wrath; and I have recompensed their deeds on their own heads" (v. 31). Intercession, quite obviously, could have made history go in a much more positive direction.

Such was the case years before when Moses came down from the mountain and found that the Israelites were worshiping a golden calf that they had made. God was so furious that He had decided to destroy all the Israelites, but He didn't. Why? Because Moses became a strategic intercessor! "Therefore He [God] said that He would destroy them, had not Moses His chosen one stood before Him in the breach, to turn away His wrath, lest He destroy them" (Ps. 106:23).

Petition and Proclamation

Let's look more closely at this intercessory event involving Moses in order to distinguish between two modes of intercession: petition mode and proclamation mode.

The petition mode of intercession is the most common. It was the one that Moses actually used when he came down from the mountain. He said to the Lord, "Oh, these people have committed a great sin, and have made for themselves a god of gold! Yet now, if You will forgive their sin—but if not, I pray, blot me out of Your book which You have written" (Exod. 32:31-32). Moses humbly begged (petitioned) God to forgive the Israelites. And, because it was effective and powerful intercession, God did.

An example of proclamation, the other mode of intercession, is the incident of Elijah confronting King Ahab. Ahab's idolatry seemed worse than the Israelites' if we take it at face value: "Ahab did more to provoke the Lord God of Israel to anger than all the kings of Israel who were before him" (1 Kings 16:33). So, the servant of the Lord, Elijah, took action, and that action was a proclamation, not a petition. He said to Ahab, "As the Lord God of Israel lives, before whom I stand, there shall not be dew nor rain these years, *except at my word*" (17:1, emphasis added). This is a remarkable statement. The outcome of this encounter now hinged on Elijah's word, not God's. God had delegated to Elijah this extraordinary degree of authority to deal with history. Elijah told Ahab that it would not rain until he gave nature permission. He did not say that it would rain only if (or when) God wills. It was Elijah's decision.

God Delegates Authority

As I see it now (on this side of my seminary days, to be sure), God continues to do similar things today. He delegates awesome authority to strategic prophetic intercessors in this paradigm, the new wineskin of the Church.

In the old wineskin, intercession was, by and large, petition only. Our prayers usually carried the tag line "If it be Your will." Why? Most of us operated under the assumption that, as mere human beings, we could not presume to know the will of God. We were taught that His ways are higher than our ways. Prayer was mostly one-way prayer, which is good, but room must be left for other kinds of prayer as well.

In the new wineskin, we have begun to add proclamation to petition. This is rooted in two-way prayer. We now believe that

God actually speaks to us! And sometimes God tells us what He desires to do in a certain situation. When He does, and when we are sure that we have heard God's voice as did Elijah, we can then *proclaim* the will of God, rather than say, "If it is Your will."

Richard Foster puts it this way:

> We are calling forth the will of the Father upon the earth. Here we are not so much speaking *to* God as speaking *for* God. We are not asking God to do something: rather, we are using the authority of God to command something done.[9]

In order to see how this works out in real life, let me give three recent examples.

Chuck Pierce

Chuck Pierce, my longtime colleague, is the apostolic leader of the United States Strategic Prayer Network (USSPN). Over a 14-month period bridging 2003 and 2004, he, along with Dutch Sheets, went on a 50-state tour in which he held meetings to rally intercessors and apostles in each state. When they arrived in California in the spring of 2003, the state was in political disarray. The intercessors had been praying fervently that something would happen to set the state on a better course. The USSPN meeting was in the state capital, Sacramento. During the meeting, Chuck Pierce heard from God. He boldly proclaimed to the audience, "The government of California will change by this fall!"

It was a bold declaration because, at that time, the matter of recalling Governor Gray Davis had not yet been discussed in the media. Nevertheless, by the fall of 2003, Davis had been recalled, and Arnold Schwarzenegger became the new governor of California.

Sunday Adelaja

Sunday Adelaja is a Nigerian friend of mine who founded and pastors what is at this writing the largest church in all of Europe in Kiev, Ukraine. A couple of years ago, the President of Ukraine and other government officials invited a psychic from another nation to come and "help" the nation. This psychic was soon casting his spells on national television on a continuous basis. Sunday locked himself up for seven days of prayer and fasting to hear the word of the Lord. When he had heard from God, he made an apostolic proclamation to the psychic through the television screen that he would be removed from Ukraine!

It so happened that the next week, Sunday Adelaja saw the psychic at a government-sponsored social event. They introduced themselves to each other and exchanged some pleasantries. Then Sunday looked him squarely in the eyes and said sharply (in English), "Come out of him, Satan!" Shortly thereafter, none of the psychic's predictions worked as they used to work. He soon shut his office in Kiev and left Ukraine for good.

Peter Wagner

I hope I will be pardoned for using myself as the final example of the proclamation mode of intercession. I was leading a gathering of 2,500 intercessors representing the International Strategic Prayer Network (ISSPN) in Hannover, Germany, in 2001. While we were in Hannover, Doris and I, as is our habit, frequented some of the distinguished steak houses in the city. I was amazed that each one we went to stated specifically on the menu that their beef was American or Argentine, but not German. I suddenly realized that this was because Germany had been plagued with mad cow disease, and consequently Germans could not even eat their own beef.

This came to mind during one of our sessions on October 1, 2001. I suddenly sensed a personal visitation from God, and

I became acutely incensed that Germans could not eat their own beef. God commanded me to go the platform, and as I unburdened myself, I began to weep profusely. When I regained control, I made an apostolic proclamation, in the name of the Lord, that mad cow disease in Europe would immediately stop! A month later a friend sent me a newspaper article from England stating that the last recorded case of mad cow disease was in September 30, 2001!

While we need to continue petitioning God in our intercessory prayers, we also need to be tuned in to what the Spirit is saying to the churches about strategic proclamation. It is powerful!

"I Was Going to Kill You!"

I want to conclude this chapter on powerful prayer with an example from the lives of my friends Eddie and Alice Smith, two of the household names in the United States prayer movement. In fact, Alice is one of Doris's and my closest personal intercessors.

When Alice was shopping in a supermarket one day, she had a vision while waiting in line at the checkout stand. In her vision, she clearly saw someone pointing a gun at Eddie in his church office! As many intercessors would, she reacted immediately. Leaving her basket of groceries, she rushed out of the store, drove home and closed herself in her prayer closet. Thirty minutes later, she felt a release. She telephoned her husband and said, "Eddie, are you okay?"

Eddie said, "Yes, I'm okay. He just got saved!"

What happened? A medical doctor who had been battling demons had loaded his pistol that day and left home to visit Pastor Eddie, whom he did not like. No sooner had he entered the church office than he realized that, unexplainably, he had left home so rapidly that he had forgotten to take his weapon off the kitchen counter. He soon confessed to Eddie, "I was going to kill you and then kill myself!" But, due to Alice's prayer, he ended up a child of God.

Is that powerful prayer or what?

Notes

1. Francis Frangipane, *The House of the Lord* (Lake Mary, FL: Creation House, 1991), pp. 56-57.
2. Brother Andrew, *And God Changed His Mind* (Old Tappan, NJ: Chosen Books, 1999), pp. 11-12.
3. Ibid., p. 12. Italics in original.
4. Richard J. Foster, *Celebration of Discipline* (San Francisco: HarperSanFrancisco, 1988), p. 35.
5. Gregory A. Boyd, *God of the Possible* (Grand Rapids, MI: Baker Books, 2000), p. 7. Italics in original.
6. John Sanders, "Does God Know Your Next Move?" *Christianity Today* (June 11, 2001), p. 52.
7. Foster, *Celebration of Discipline*, p. 35.
8. Walter Wink, "Prayer and the Powers," *Sojourners* (October 1990), p. 10.
9. Richard J. Foster, *Prayer: Finding the Heart's True Home* (San Francisco: HarperSanFrancisco, 1992), p. 229.

PRINCIPLE NO. 7

Tuning In to New Levels of Power

This concluding chapter will be somewhat different from the others. The first six principles, including the operational role of the Holy Spirit, warfare worship, prophecy, miraculous healing, demonic deliverance and powerful prayer were all emphases that were actually present in some churches while I was being trained in seminary. However, the seminaries I attended were not tuned in to that segment of the Body of Christ. In fact, the more vocal and aggressive leaders of such churches were often dismissed, as I have mentioned previously, as the lunatic fringe by some of my professors. I was taught that respectable Christians did not get involved in such things or associate with those who did.

New Power Levels

Neither this book on power principles nor any other like it could possibly be the final word on the subject because God's work here on Earth is not yet complete. We can write about power principles that we are currently aware of, but it would be foolish to think that God has finished revealing all the power principles that He is ever going to reveal.

In my opinion, some Christian leaders today are a bit too nostalgic about the first century. This is not surprising, because the New Testament, from which we derive all the basic principles for our Christian lives and ministries, was revealed to people during the first century.

There is no question that the Bible is the only divinely inspired book that we have. It is easy, however, to be swept away by our admiration for the believers in the first century. For example, I frequently hear the cry that what we need to correct the flaws of our churches today is to make them "first-century" churches. I know it will surprise some people when I say that I couldn't disagree more. Who would want their church to be like the Corinthian church? Or the Galatian church? Or the Laodicean church? While we can and should learn from the past, I don't believe that our future should be subject to our past. I think that what we need today are biblical, *twenty-first*-century churches if we are going to win people to Christ and transform our communities.

Hearing New Things from the Holy Spirit

Nothing in the New Testament says that we should stagnate, live in the past or be satisfied with the status quo. In fact, the New Testament says quite the contrary. Paul writes:

> Forgetting those things which are behind and reaching forward to those things which are ahead, I press toward the goal for the prize of the upward call of God in Christ Jesus (Phil. 3:13-14).

Paul knew that he could not move into his God-appointed destiny with a vision focused on the past. His vision was to press on to God's call for the future.

One of the devil's most subtle attacks against God's people comes in the form of the spirit of religion. The spirit of religion is an agent of Satan assigned to prevent change and to maintain the status quo by using religious devices. This religious spirit tries to force us to look backward, not forward.

Jesus' teaching that God provides new wineskins for the new things that He does is very important to understand and to take seriously (see Matt. 9:17). God is decisively pouring out new wine here in the twenty-first century that first-century wineskins were not designed to hold. This is why the Bible says, "He who has an ear, let him hear what the Spirit says to the churches" (Rev. 2:11).

The word "says" in this verse is in present tense. We certainly should be aware of what the Spirit has said to the churches through the ages, but it is even more important for us to hear what the Spirit is saying to us today. There is no valid biblical assumption that the Holy Spirit never says anything new. On the contrary, I believe that the Holy Spirit continually says important things to each new generation that He did not say to previous generations.

Let's Not Be Pharisees!

The Pharisees did not like Jesus' new wineskins. The spirit of religion had such a tight grip on them that they dedicated their lives to prevent God's new times and seasons from being realized. The Pharisees were not bad people. They strictly followed the laws of God. They were respected leaders of the Jews. Why, then, did they hate Jesus so much? It was because Jesus came to bring a new season—the kingdom of God. Even though He was the Messiah that they had been waiting for over the centuries, they could not see it because the religious spirit had effectively blinded their eyes.

One of the telling confrontations came when the Pharisees once asked Jesus, "Why do Your disciples transgress the tradition of the elders? For they do not wash their hands when they eat bread" (Matt. 15:2). This was not an issue of violating the Ten Commandments. This was the "tradition of the elders," which means that over time the religious leaders of Israel had added layer after layer of religious tradition to the Law, introducing a legalism that kept people away from God rather than drawing them closer to God. The Pharisees were so committed to their religion that they felt that anyone who did not do as they did offended God. They sincerely thought that they were doing the will of God. In reality, they were being victimized by the spirit of religion.

Jesus, of course, saw through this. His response to the Pharisees was, "Why do you also transgress the commandment of God because of your tradition?" (v. 3). The spirit of religion can become so powerful that those under its influence are not just benignly neutral, but also allow themselves to get into a position in which they actually work against God. Ordinarily, if you try to tell this to these individuals, they won't hear you because their minds have been so twisted by that demon that they think they are doing God's will.

Jesus showed the Pharisees how they had twisted a specific commandment of God and called them "hypocrites" (v. 7). Then He said, "In vain they worship Me, teaching as doctrines the commandments of men" (v. 9). Two thousand years later, religious leaders are still teaching religious rules and regulations produced by human beings as if they were absolute doctrines. The spirit of religion that affected the Pharisees still affects pastors, ministry leaders, teachers, denominational executives and many others today. The Holy Spirit is speaking to the churches about power ministries, but many do not want to follow the new directions. They prefer to remain in their comfort zones.

Five Newly Revealed Power Principles

Part of what God expects of us is to tune in to the new things that He is constantly revealing, in this case the new power principles that He is opening up to us. In this chapter, I will list five of these principles that I didn't learn about in seminary. But this time, the reason that I didn't learn these power principles in seminary is because the Spirit had not yet spoken to the churches about them.

Before I list these five new power principles, let me first say that these five do not complete the list. They will help us catch up a bit, but God will not be finished revealing new things, designing new wineskins and moving us into new times and seasons until Jesus returns. In the days to come, I do not doubt that believers will be using awesome power principles that I could not list today. This should be expected, for as Jesus said, "He who believes in Me, the works that I do he will do also; and greater works than these he will do, because I go to My Father" (John 14:12).

While I didn't learn these five power principles when I went to seminary, I did have the privilege of teaching them to my students at Fuller Seminary in the 1990s, and I am currently teaching them to my students at the Wagner Leadership Institute.

I consider them to be the five most important new concepts related to power ministries that the Holy Spirit revealed to the churches in the 1990s. My goal here is simply to describe the concepts and to guide you to some up-to-date resources, which will give you the additional details you need to incorporate them into your ministry for God.

1. Strategic-Level Spiritual Warfare

It was back during the legendary international congress on evangelism in Manila, called Lausanne II, in which the concept of "territorial spirits" became known to the wider Body of Christ. That was 1989, the threshold year into the decade of the 1990s. Prior to this congress in Manila, very few Christian leaders had even heard about territorial spirits. But during the congress, five speakers, who chose their own topics, spoke about those high-ranking principalities and how they could obstruct world evangelization.

While in Manila, I sensed that God was saying to me, "Take leadership in the area of territorial spirits." So, I began to gather others around me who believed that this was something the Spirit was truly saying to the churches, and we organized the Spiritual Warfare Network in 1990. Our objective was to process together what we were hearing and to communicate it to the wider Body of Christ. My role was to serve as the International Coordinator of the Spiritual Warfare Network. We held invitation-only meetings through 1993, and then went public with a national conference in 1994. Subsequently, the name of the organization was changed from the Spiritual Warfare Network to the Strategic Prayer Network.

During those early meetings, we developed technical terms for three different categories of spiritual warfare:

1. **Ground-level spiritual warfare.** This is the ministry of deliverance or casting out demons from individuals.
2. **Occult-level spiritual warfare.** This involves confronting more organized forces of evil in areas such as witchcraft, satanism, voodoo, Eastern religions, Freemasonry, Santería, magic and New Age.
3. **Strategic-level spiritual warfare.** This has to do with neutralizing the power of territorial and other kinds of high-ranking spirits whose assignment from Satan is to block the progress of world evangelization.

Not surprisingly, God began to reveal this in an international congress on *evangelism*. Strategic-level spiritual warfare emerges from Paul's teaching as the reason that more people are not being saved, for "the god of this age" has blinded their minds (see 2 Cor. 4:4). In order to keep people in darkness, Satan has deployed a whole hierarchy of demonic principalities and powers, the highest members of which have been assigned cities, nations, people groups, religions, neighborhoods, industries or other social networks that bind human beings together.

Our marching orders for helping to open up these people to the gospel do not involve wrestling "against flesh and blood, but against principalities, against powers, against the rulers of the darkness of this age" (Eph. 6:12). The testing ground for this new power principle was the AD2000 Movement, which operated during the 1990s. The AD2000 Movement is now regarded as the largest and most comprehensive united evangelistic movement seen to date. The focus was on the unreached peoples of the 10/40 Window. I was invited to coordinate the Movement's United Prayer Track, and I brought the Spiritual Warfare Network with me. We entered into an intense decade of strategic-level spiritual warfare.

Looking back, the results speak for themselves. The logarithmic escalation of the Christian movement in nations such as China, India, Indonesia, Nigeria, Nepal and other 10/40 Window nations is now a matter of record. At the beginning of the decade, we counted 1,739 significantly large unreached people groups, and by the end of the decade, the number had been reduced to 500. Despite a persistent Christian anti-spiritual warfare movement, the Body of Christ has emerged understanding the power of strategic-level spiritual warfare.

Resources that I highly recommend include *Possessing the Gates of the Enemy* by Cindy Jacobs, *The Jericho Hour* by Dick Eastman, *Shaking the Heavens* by Ana Méndez, and *Authority to Tread* by Rebecca Greenwood.

2. Spiritual Mapping

The pioneer in the field of spiritual mapping is George Otis, Jr. Spiritual mapping can be seen as the principal research component of strategic-level spiritual warfare. We know that the weapons of our warfare are not carnal, but spiritual (see 2 Cor. 10:4). Our major spiritual weapon is powerful prayer, and the more targeted our prayers, the more powerful they can be. Spiritual mapping helps us target our prayers accurately. There is little use in spending our time with vague, scattered shotgun prayers when we can use the same amount of time for accurate, rifle shot prayers against the enemy.

But in order to do this, we need to know as much about our enemy and his tactics as we can. No respectable general sends troops into battle without the best intelligence. If we hope to push back territorial spirits so that people under their influence

THE HOLY SPIRIT IS SPEAKING TO THE CHURCHES ABOUT POWER MINISTRIES, BUT MANY DO NOT WANT TO FOLLOW THE NEW DIRECTIONS. THEY PREFER TO REMAIN IN THEIR COMFORT ZONES.

can hear the gospel, it is imperative to have accurate knowledge of what we are up against.

As I have mentioned more than once, the Bible says, "Lest Satan should take advantage of us; for we are not ignorant of his devices" (2 Cor. 2:11). If we *are* ignorant of Satan's devices, obviously he will take advantage of us! Too many people are taken advantage of in our cities today. Spiritual mapping helps to reduce our level of ignorance and therefore our level of vulnerability.

Spiritual mapping is to intercessors what X-rays or MRIs are to surgeons. No surgeon would want to cut blindly when the best medical technology can show him or her exactly where to cut. The same applies to spiritual mapping. It opens the door for incredible new power on the part of intercessors.

The United States Strategic Prayer Network (USSPN), under the leadership of Chuck Pierce, takes spiritual mapping very seriously. Each one of the

50 USSPN state coordinators is responsible for generating and storing the spiritual mapping of their state. This becomes an invaluable resource for prophetic intercessors who are determined to see social transformation come to their regions.

For resources in this area, George Otis, Jr., has written several books, but his classic is *Informed Intercession*. If you read only one book on spiritual mapping, read this one. For years to come, it will be our official textbook on the subject. Another interesting and informative book is one that I edited, *Breaking Strongholds in Your City*. It has several chapters by experts in the field such as Bob Beckett, Harold Caballeros, Cindy Jacobs, Victor Lorenzo and Kjell Sjoberg, in addition to George Otis and me. It also has a list of 60 important questions to ask when you undertake the spiritual mapping of a particular place. These questions are divided into historical questions, physical questions and spiritual questions.

3. Identificational Repentance

The basic methodology of spiritual mapping involves three questions:

1. What is wrong with our community?
2. How did it get that way?
3. What can we do about it?

Granted, these are not simple questions to answer, especially the one that asks how our communities got that way. But when you use the resources mentioned in the last section and apply the principles of spiritual mapping, you will find that the invisible world has a great deal of influence on the visible world—much more than people ordinarily think. Spiritual mapping is seeing things as they *really* are, not as they *appear* to be.

Almost invariably, your spiritual mapping will turn up the fact that, sometime in the near or more distant past, your community, *as a community,* has sinned. You will also find that it usually has sinned not just once, but multiple times. These corporate sins leave behind wounds, which can become openings for high-level demonic forces to invade and influence the whole community. Discovering this fact will help you understand how your community got the way that it is.

What, then, can we do about it? In the 1990s, God raised John Dawson up to pioneer the field of identificational repentance. Once the sins of the past have been uncovered, those of us alive today and identified with the community have the authority to repent of these sins, and the blood of Jesus can remit them. I am not speaking of *individual* sins, but of *corporate* sins.

How powerful can identificational repentance be? If done wisely, it can tear down strongholds that the enemy has been using to permeate and control our communities for decades and even centuries. Once that happens, the power of God can be released through prayer and spiritual warfare to stop Satan's evil work of stealing, killing and destroying! It also can help open doors to receiving God's blessing for city transformation.

The recognized textbook for identificational repentance is John Dawson's *Healing America's Wounds.* I also highly recommend John Sandford's *Healing the Nations,* Jim Goll's *Father Forgive Us!* and *Sins of the Fathers* by Brian Mills and Roger Mitchell.

4. Territorial Commitment

New apostolic pastors, more frequently than traditional pastors, tend to sense a lifetime call to their churches and to their communities. The churches they pastor are ordinarily not seen as a mere stepping-stone for moving on to larger churches somewhere else, because the pastors typically feel called to their churches for life. This allows pastors to rise to a level of spiritual authority in their communities that they could not otherwise attain. It is called "territorial commitment," and this is now recognized as a crucial power principle for city transformation.

Bob Beckett, pastor of the Dwelling Place Church in Hemet, California, was the human instrument that God used to bring territorial commitment to the attention of the Body of Christ in the 1990s. For years after he planted the Dwelling Place Church, it was a mess. It hardly grew. He experienced five major church splits. There were no finances even for small projects like remodeling the nursery. The pastors in the city were indifferent toward the ministry of other pastors in the city. Bob and the congregation of the Dwelling Place Church prayed fervently that a visitation of God would come to the city of Hemet, but to no avail.

Then, through a series of personal revelations, Bob and his wife, Susan, felt the call of God to commit themselves to spending the rest of their lives in Hemet, no matter what. They sealed their decision by purchasing a cemetery plot, and they displayed the deed to the congregation the next Sunday along with the promise that they would stay.

The situation changed immediately! The church began to grow and has now moved into a new, modern worship center. Bob is honored as a leader in the church, and there have been no more church splits. The pastors in the city now love each other and support each other. And the city of Hemet itself has seen tangible signs of social transformation. Commitment to a territory definitely can make a difference.

The groundbreaking book for territorial commitment is *Commitment to Conquer* by Bob Beckett. Bob Beckett and the city of Hemet, California, are featured in the monumental video

Transformations by George Otis, Jr. The major textbook in the field is *Releasing Heaven on Earth: God's Principles for Restoring the Land* by Alistair Petrie.

5. Prophetic Acts

Of all the newer forms of power ministries that the Holy Spirit has been bringing to the attention of the Church, I have noticed that prophetic acts are possibly the scariest to some. Admittedly, prophetic acts are high-risk activities. Consequently, they tend to take many out of their comfort zones. They often look really strange—so strange that those who participate in them might be considered by others as mentally challenged.

There is no denying that some prophetic acts (not all) push the boundaries of what we consider normal human behavior. However, many of these types of prophetic acts are recorded approvingly in the Bible. For example:

- **Isaiah walked around naked for three years.** The reason? God said, "Just as My servant Isaiah has walked naked and barefoot three years for a sign and a wonder against Egypt and Ethiopia, so shall the king of Assyria lead away the Egyptians as prisoners and the Ethiopians as captives, young and old, naked and barefoot, with their buttocks uncovered, to the shame of Egypt" (Isa. 20:3-4).
- **Jeremiah buried his underwear.** Here is how Jeremiah tells the story: "God told me, 'Go and buy yourself some linen shorts. Put them on and keep them on. Don't even take them off to wash them.' So I bought the shorts as God directed and put them on. Then God told me, 'Take the shorts that you bought

and go straight to Perath and hide them there in a crack in the rock.' So I did what God told me and hid them at Perath. Next, after quite a long time, God told me, 'Go back to Perath and get the linen shorts I told you to hide there.' So I went back to Perath and dug them out of the place where I had hidden them. The shorts by then had rotted and were worthless" (Jer. 13:1-7, *THE MESSAGE*). What was the purpose? To show Israel and Judah that they had become worthless because of idolatry.

- **Ezekiel shaved his head and beard.** The Lord said, "And you, son of man, take a sharp sword, take it as a barber's razor, and pass it over your head and your beard; then take scales to weigh and divide the hair. You shall burn with fire one-third in the midst of the city, when the days of the siege are finished; then you shall take one-third and strike around it with the sword, and one-third you shall scatter in the wind: I will draw out a sword after them" (Ezek. 5:1-2). This was an introduction to the ways that God was going to judge Jerusalem.

What was going on? Here is the way Dutch Sheets explains prophetic acts:

> Prophetic action or declaration is something said or done in the natural realm at the direction of God that prepares the way for Him to move in the spiritual realm, which then consequently effects change in the natural realm. How's that for God and man partnering? God says to do or say something. We obey. Our words or actions impact the heavenly realm, which then impacts the natural realm.[1]

Notice the phrase "at the direction of God" in Dutch Sheets's definition. Each prophetic act, like those of Isaiah, Jeremiah and Ezekiel, must be done only because we clearly hear from God. This flashes back to issues that we dealt with in previous chapters on prophecy and powerful prayer. We can receive God's direction by two-way prayer. It can also come through illumination of the Holy Spirit as we read God's Word. It can come through a prophetic word that we receive from another. Prophetic acts are not human designs or creative methodologies. If they are, they can easily backfire. God's guidance and His anointing are essential.

As Dutch Sheets says, prophetic acts have the power to shift things in the invisible world, so that God does things that He would not do otherwise. This is not a statement relating to God's sovereignty or His omnipotence; it is simply a statement of how the sovereign God has decided to arrange the universe He created.

Moses' Rod

For example, think of Moses' rod. The rod was not a magical wand that had power in itself; it was just a stick of wood. The rod did not manipulate supernatural power like a witch's incantation. Yet when Moses used that rod and performed a prophetic act on the banks of the Red Sea, power came from the invisible world that allowed the Israelites to travel on dry land, and the same power drowned the pursuing Egyptian army.

So, here is the obvious question: What if Moses had decided, for whatever reason, not to do the prophetic act and lift his rod? The most straightforward reading of the Scripture would lead one to believe that, in such a case, the Egyptians would have overtaken the Israelites and history would have been quite different. Calvinistic theologians with a strong commitment to predestination would have difficulty in even entertaining the possibility. But not open theists such as I quoted in the last chapter. In *Prayer*

Is Invading the Impossible, Jack Hayford says, "You and I can help decide which of these two things—blessing or cursing—happens on earth. We will determine whether God's goodness is released toward specific situations or whether the power of sin and Satan is permitted to prevail."[2]

Cali, Colombia

To bring this into our world, let's look at a prophetic act done by my friend Randy MacMillan, a missionary to Cali, Colombia. Back in 1996, a notorious drug cartel had control of the city of Cali. Randy called his church to a three-day, nonstop prayer vigil with the explicit purpose of binding the strongman over Cali. The strongman was a drug lord named José Santiago.

At the end of the three-day prayer offensive, Randy and his church received direction from God to do a prophetic act, which they obeyed explicitly. On Sunday night, March 3, 1996, they filled empty plastic ketchup containers with three gallons of olive oil. They got in their cars and sprinkled olive oil around the city limits, around city hall and around José Santiago's residence.

The next day, the police, after years of frustration, captured and killed Santiago. The headline in the following day's newspaper was, "Cayó el Hombre Fuerte del Cartel de Cali!" or "The Strongman Over Cali's Drug Cartel Has Fallen!" Would this have happened if Randy MacMillan's team had not sprinkled the three gallons of olive oil? Would the Red Sea have parted if Moses had not raised his rod?

Conclusion

I have referred to seminaries quite a bit in this book. In the final analysis, however, what people learned or did not learn in seminary actually matters very little in comparison to having an ear for hearing what the Spirit is continually saying to the churches right now. My prayer is that the apostolic power principles that you have learned about in this book will enable you, your friends and your church to move to new levels in doing your part to advance the kingdom of God and to bring glory to Jesus Christ!

Notes

1. Dutch Sheets, *Intercessory Prayer* (Ventura, CA: Regal Books, 1996), p. 220.
2. Jack W. Hayford, *Prayer Is Invading the Impossible* (New York: Ballantine Books, 1990), p. 57.

Recommended Resources

Beckett, Bob. *Commitment to Conquer.* Grand Rapids, MI: Chosen Books, 1997.
Brother Andrew with Susan DeVore Williams. *And God Changed His Mind.* Grand Rapids, MI: Chosen Books, 1999.
Dawson, John. *Healing America's Wounds.* Ventura, CA: Regal Books, 1994.
Deere, Jack. *Surprised by the Power of the Spirit.* Grand Rapids, MI: Zondervan Publishing House, 1993.
——. *Surprised by the Voice of God.* Grand Rapids, MI: Zondervan Publishing House, 1998.
Eastman, Dick. *The Jericho Hour.* Lake Mary, FL: Creation House, 1994.
Goll, Jim. *Father Forgive Us!* Shippensburg, PA: Destiny Image Publishers, 1999.
Greenwood, Rebecca. *Authority to Tread.* Lake Mary, FL: Chosen Books, 2005.
Griffith, Jill. *How to Have a Dynamic Church Prayer Ministry.* Colorado Springs, CO: Wagner Publications, 1999.
Hamon, Bill. *Prophets and Personal Prophecy.* Shippensburg, PA: Destiny Image Publishers, 1987.
Hayford, Jack. *Prayer Is Invading the Impossible.* New York: Ballantine Books, 1990.
Jacobs, Cindy. *Possessing the Gates of the Enemy.* Grand Rapids, MI: Chosen Books, 1994.
——. *The Voice of God.* Ventura, CA: Regal Books, 1995.
Maxwell, John. *Partners in Prayer.* Nashville, TN: Thomas Nelson, 1996.
Méndez, Ana. *Shaking the Heavens.* Ventura, CA: Renew Books, 2000.
Mills, Brian and Roger Mitchell. *Sins of the Fathers.* Tonbridge, United Kingdom: Sovereign World, 1999.
Otis, George Jr. *Informed Intercession.* Ventura, CA: Renew Books, 1999.
——. *Transformations.* VHS. Lynnwood, WA: The Sentinel Group, 1999.

Petrie, Alistair. *Releasing Heaven on Earth: God's Principles for Restoring the Land.* Lake Mary, FL: Chosen Books, 2000.

Sandford, John. *Healing the Nations.* Lake Mary, FL: Chosen Books, 2000.

Teykl, Terry. *Making Room to Pray*. Muncie, IN: Prayer Point Press, 1999.

——. *Your Pastor: Preyed On or Prayed For.* Muncie, IN: Prayer Point Press, 2000.

Wagner, C. Peter, ed. *Breaking Strongholds in Your City.* Ventura, CA: Regal Books, 1993.

——. *Look Out! The Pentecostals Are Coming.* Lake Mary, FL: Creation House, 1973.

——. *Prayer Shield.* Ventura, CA: Regal Books, 1992.

——. *Your Spiritual Gifts Can Help Your Church Grow.* Ventura, CA: Regal Books, 2005.

Scripture Index

Subject Index